Florida Marine Shells

Florida
MARINE SHELLS

A Guide
for Collectors of Shells of the Southeastern Atlantic Coast and Gulf Coast

by C. N. VILAS
and N. R. VILAS

Diagrams by N. R. VILAS

CHARLES E. TUTTLE COMPANY: PUBLISHERS
Rutland, Vermont & Tokyo, Japan

Representatives
Continental Europe: BOXERBOOKS, INC., *Zurich*
British Isles: PRENTICE-HALL INTERNATIONAL, INC., *London*
Australasia: PAUL FLESCH & CO., PTY. LTD., *Melbourne*
Canada: M. G. HURTIG LTD., *Edmonton*

Published by the Charles E. Tuttle Company, Inc.
of Rutland, Vermont & Tokyo, Japan
with editorial offices at
Suido 1-chome, 2–6, Bunkyo-ku, Tokyo, Japan

Copyright in Japan, 1970 by Charles E. Tuttle Co., Inc.

Library of Congress Catalog Card No. 72-109421

Standard Book No. 8048 0883-x

First Tuttle edition published 1970

PRINTED IN JAPAN

TABLE OF CONTENTS

Build thee more stately mansions, O my soul,
As the swift seasons roll!
Leave thy low-vaulted past!
Let each new temple, nobler than the last,
Shut thee from heaven with a dome more vast,
Till thou at length art free,
Leaving thine outgrown shell by life's unresting sea!

Oliver Wendell Holmes: *The Chambered Nautilus*. Stanza 5.

INTRODUCTION

Gather a shell from the strown beach
And listen at its lips: they sigh
The same desire and mystery,
The echo of the whole sea's speech.
Dante Gabriel Rossetti: *The
Sea Limits.* Stanza 4.
Listen thou well, for my shell hath speech.
Charles Henry Webb: *With a
Nantucket Shell*

Marine mollusks! They are so compelling; emotionally so fascinating, intellectually so instructive. Their striking features will tingle our artistic taste, appeal to our sense of beauty—their rhythmic forms, their varied sculpture, their vivid colors, their romantic histories. Do we wish that these forms could speak? Their sounds are not silent; in tuned tones they sing the songs and sagas of the sea. These countless forms that charm our eyes are full of meaning, and move us to comprehend something of their place and purpose in the scheme of God's great outdoors.

Just as the enjoyment of a trip to a foreign country is greatly enhanced by preliminary knowledge of the history, habits, customs, and language of the people; so also a trip to a sea beach is rendered more intelligible by preliminary knowledge of the history, habits, structure, and beauty of the elaborate shells which delight a collector on the seashore. It has been the aim of the authors to design a book which would serve a preparatory purpose—a book which would instruct the amateur collector without being too technical; aid in the identification of the most common shells without creating confusion; present a conception of the living mollusk; and create a substantial interest in shell collecting by means of colored illustrations, concise descriptions, clear basic classification, and general scientific facts. In short, *Florida Marine Shells* is to be a guide for amateur shell collectors whether at home or on the wave-washed beaches.

The book is believed to possess a high degree of accuracy since the study collection was carefully made and checked, and the sources of information were authentic and of recent writing or revision.

It gives us much pleasure to acknowledge the scientific assistance and inspirational suggestions we have received from Dr. Fritz Haas. Chicago Natural History Museums, Chicago, Illinois.

In retiring from this interesting enterprise, we wish to give due thanks to all who have aided us either in suggestions or assistance; and particularly to those supporters of shell collecting who have believed enough in the need for this book to promote its production.

CURTIS N. VILAS

NAOMI R. VILAS

Osprey, Florida

PREFACE TO THE SECOND EDITION

In this new edition the basic text has been checked for accuracy and the nomenclature brought up to date in accord with modern check lists of shell names. The chief purpose of this second edition has been to include as many more illustrations and descriptions of additional species as space and circumstances would permit. To admit more species simply because they are known to exist, without assurance that the general collector would readily find them, was aside from the basis of selection. It has seemed desirable to include in this guide for amateur collectors only those species which have been found as living mollusks in reasonably accessible locations.

In order to cover a more natural shell area and to make the book more valuable to a greater number of users, the following explanation is made as to the geographic limits of species included in this book. It may be expected that all species described can be found in some part of the coastal region which extends along the southeastern coast of North America from North Carolina south to the Florida Keys and west to Texas.

The index, an indispensable feature with its cross-references, has been enlarged to include all additional species. For aid in determining the millimeter length as well as inch length of specimens, a measuring scale has been added.

The authors hope that this book which has given so much pleasure and assistance to collectors in the past may still serve as a practical guide for all newcomers in this branch of natural science.

CURTIS N. VILAS
NAOMI R. VILAS

Osprey, Florida

SHELL COLLECTING

Countless creatures of incredible beauty and fantasy crowd the Florida beaches, and at the same time keep themselves so well concealed that it takes a keen observer to find their hidden homes. Their interesting habits are sure to create curiosity and fascinate an observer. To discover these marine creatures, to learn the meaning of their forms and habits, to reflect upon their systematic order and relationship in the realm of nature, directs one toward the field of naturalistic science. But apart from the philosophical phase and scientific side of shell collecting, the casual naturalist is delighted with the pleasant pastime of simply observing the pretty shells and marine creatures that appear at his feet while walking on the Florida beaches.

Low tide is the most favorable time for collecting. At that time many objects are exposed and places made accessible which are not apparent at other times. The times of the new and full moon result in an unusually low ebb tide. These times provide occasions for exploring molluscan stations which are not easily accessible at ordinary low tides. Beach collecting is also especially profitable after storms because many deep water specimens are torn from their stations and tossed high up on the beach either as live specimens or very fresh dead ones.

Florida provides a countless number and variety of interesting collection centers. The outline map of Florida in this edition will serve to locate the main collection centers and show the relationship of one center to another. Regions which are especially rich in a variety of species and individuals are St. Petersburg, Sarasota, Sanibel Island, Bonita Springs, Key West, middle Florida Keys, Biscayne Bay, Lake Worth, and Jupiter Inlet. Most people are so situated that they can not explore all centers. This should not be discouraging even to an enthusiastic shell collector, for most gratifying collecting comes from concentrating on one center. If any person who is situated close to a good collecting center acquires a clear understanding of molluscan stations and habits, takes advantage of varying weather and wave condition, and makes frequent and extended trips to a given field, he will be amply rewarded with a variety of rare as well as common specimens; for shells of nearly all marine mollusks of reasonable depth can be found at one time or another on beaches. Trips to a variety of beaches are usually too short and occasional to be satisfactory and profitable.

It is important to know where to look for beach specimens. For example, small fragile shells are usually found after a calm tide high up on the beach in the ridge of debris left by the receding tide. Large shells are more apt to be found at the high tide line with coarse debris. Minute specimens or boring species are often found attached to or within seaweeds, sponges, broken shells, pieces of timber and bits of coral. All such debris tossed up or deposited by the tide waters is worth examining.

Successful shell collecting, other than the beach collecting just discussed, depends largely upon a knowledge of specific molluscan stations—a term used to refer to the kind of external surroundings in which a given mollusk is best adapted to carry on its life functions. It is so customary for a given molluscan species to have a particular combination of environmental conditions that it is useless to look for living specimens except in their selected localities. For example, some species of *Modiolus* and *Ostrea* attach themselves to mangrove roots in bayous and salt flats; hence extremely low tide exposes them to the air. Certain species of *Barnea* should be looked for in the mud around the roots of mangrove trees. *Melampus* and *Littorina* live in brackish inside waters and marshes where they often attach themselves to old piling and concrete wharves. Salt flats, subject to tidal action are favorite places for *Polymesoda, Cerithium, Melongena, Tellina, Anomalocardia, Marginella,* and *Cerithidea.* Certain species of *Nassarius, Terebra, Natica, Polynices,* and *Urosalpinx* move about on sandy bottoms trying to detect the extended siphons of their buried prey—namely, *Venus, Macrocallista, Tellina, Chione,* and *Mactra.* At certain times *Pyrene, Cerithium, Modulus* and *Marginella* are found on grassy bottoms. *Maculopeplum, Chama. Spondylus, Trivia* and *Murex* are found on coral reefs, sponges, and exposed sections of hardpan. *Petcen gibbus irradians* is found in bays where it is very plentiful in the spring, and *Pecten gibbus* is abundant in the Gulf with the less common *Pecten ziczac* in three to four fathoms of water, but *Pecten nodosus* favors deeper water —five fathoms or more.

Some species endure a variety of depths both in bays and open Gulf waters. Notable in this group are *Strombus pugilis, Muricidea multangula. Fasciolaria gigantea. F. tulipa, F. distans, Cantharus tinctus,* and *Chione cancellata.*

Because of the Gulf Stream, Florida east coast shell species are definitely different from the west coast shells. Deeper water species, rock dwelling species, and scattered Bahama species can be expected.

Another molluscan peculiarity worth noting is the seasonal and yearly variation in quantities of individuals and kinds of species. For instance, *Fasciolaria, Pecten,* and *Murex* are abundant in shallow waters only during the spawning season. In certain years, bivalves such as *Arca occidentalis* and *Pecten muscosus* are notably numerous; and in other years they are conspicuously scarce.

Some equipment for collecting live specimens upon sandy open water beaches or in shallow inside waters is necessary: a shovel of convenient size and weight, a sieve, and a net. A convenient sieve is two feet square and four inches high. Two screens should be fastened over the bottom—a heavy wire mesh, and a fine mesh which runs about sixteen squares to the inch. A net may be bought or made by fastening a conical shaped piece of fine netting or coarse cotton material on a heavy wire hoop. This may be fastened to a handle or used without a handle. Such a net is useful in exploring around sea grasses and grassy bottoms. A sweeping motion is most effective. Additional useful equipment consists of: a pair of forceps, a strong pocket knife, a hand lens, assorted covered jars and vials for small specimens, fifty percent alcohol for preserving specimens, convenient containers for shells, and non-metal buckets in which to keep large mollusks alive.

About midway between high and low tide mark is a good place to start digging. Take a shovelful of surface soil and place it in the sieve. Sift and wash all the material thoroughly so as not to lose any interesting small species. Repeat this process several times at increasingly deeper depths in the same spot in order to find the deep burrowing species. This procedure of digging and sifting should be repeated in a variety of depths and in places where the character of the seabottom is definitely different. With a reasonable amount of experience, any amateur collector will become a skillful collector of live, hidden mollusks.

Dredging is the only method by which living mollusks can be taken in water beyond the wading limits. A few types of dredges which have been experimented with successfully are the bucket dredge, scallop dredge, and simple circular dredge made from a sewer pipe. Any type dredge is operated from a boat by means of a tow-rope which should be at least twice as long as the depth of the water in which dredging operations are being carried on. If dredging is being carried on in five fathoms or more of water, it is wise to fasten a float to the dredge to avoid losing it in case the tow-rope should break.

Dredging is a fascinating experience because excitement precedes the inspection of each dredge load. Everything should be carefully inspected because some small shells are attached to and have the same color of sea weeds, other shells are attached to rocks and broken shells, and some rare pectens are covered with and imbedded in sponge growths. Dredging, in addition to being fascinating, brings to the collector's hand live specimens which are not discovered by any other means.

Accurate data should be recorded on the spot regarding the collecting conditions. Even the most amateur collector can contribute valuable knowledge to the subject of malacology by keeping reliable records because many marine regions have not been authentically explored. Specimens without records are valueless. Notebooks and labels should be used to record the following data: Name (when known) or number, date of finding, station or locality, depth of water, water temperature, and character of sea bottom. Collections made as systematically as this should be of value not only to the collector but also to science.

Specimen shells should be cleaned properly so that shell beauty is enhanced and not destroyed, and promptly so that decomposition of animal parts and resultant unpleasant odors do not set-in. Boiling is the most satisfactory method of removing the fleshy or soft parts. Smooth and highly polished shells should not be boiled longer than two minutes. Other shells should be boiled from two to twenty minutes depending upon the size of the shell. They may be put directly into boiling water, or they may be put in warm water which is then brought to the boiling point. Cool the shells sufficiently to permit handling and then remove the fleshy parts by a careful combination of pulling and twisting. Be careful not to leave the apical tip of univalve animals in the shell. In the event that this does happen, place a few drops of alcohol in the apex of the shell for a couple of days. A hair pin or other simple sharp instrument is effective in pulling out the soft parts of small univalves. Minute specimens may be placed to dry without removing the soft parts.

The shells are now ready for surface cleaning. In many cases a stiff brush does the job satisfactorily. If calcareous structures and deposits are attached to the shells, it may be necessary to place them in a weak solution of muriatic acid or one of the commercial cleaning fluids for a few seconds. Shells left too long in an acid solution, however, will be dulled and corroded. Sometimes calcified deposits can be effectively removed with a sharp edge or pointed tool.

The hinge ligament of bivalves and epidermis of shells when present can be kept from extreme drying by soaking the shells in a solution of equal parts of glycerine and water. After being removed from the solution, the valves should be tied shut until the hinge has dried sufficiently to counteract opening.

Opercula of univalves should be glued to pieces of cotton which are pushed into the aperture of the shell so that the operculum of each univalve is placed in a natural position.

A small amount of olive oil brushed onto shell surfaces enlivens the luster and brightens the color. Shells prepared according to the above suggestions will be properly preserved and will have their full beauty revealed.

A scientific system of cabinet classification is recommended with distinct divisions of classes, families, genera, and species. Each shell should then be given a label bearing the complete species name, author's name, locality where found, and collector's name. A collection of shells displayed in such a way should be a joy to the beholder, a satisfaction to the possessor, and an asset to science.

Measuring Scale in Millimeters

Measuring Scale in Inches

Dwellers by the sea cannot fail to be impressed by the sight of its ceaseless ebb and flow, and are apt, on the principles of that rude philosophy of sympathy and resemblance . . . to trace a subtle relation, a secret harmony, between its tides and the life of man. . . . The belief that most deaths happen at ebb tide is said to be held along the east coast of England from Northumberland to Kent.

Sir James George Frazer: *The Golden Bough.*
Chapter 3

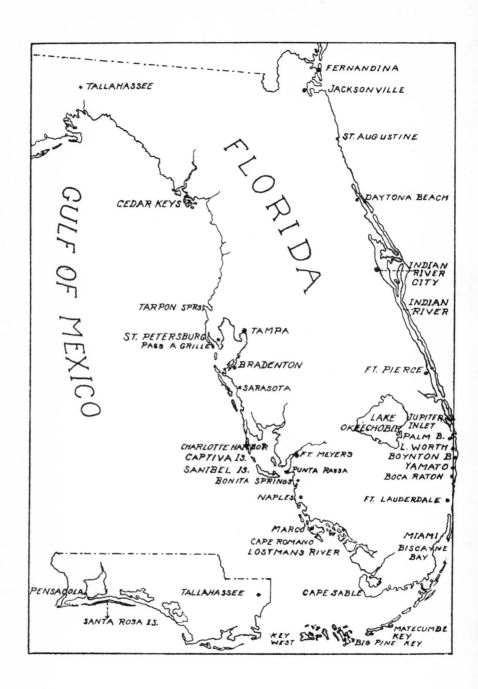

GENERAL INFORMATION ABOUT MOLLUSKS

All outlines of the evolutionary development of the earth begin with the theory that life began in the sea. The complete life cycles of those early forms were carried on in or under the water. After long ages of development, these early forms are presumed to have produced shelly or skeleton-like structures whose recognizable fossil remains in stratified deposits give clews to the character of these first forms of life. Consequently, fossil shells play an important part in piecing together the story which tells the history of life's beginning. For countless ages fossils have been known to men but only in the last century and a half has man grasped their real significance and intelligently used them to solve the mystery of life's earliest nature and history. Florida's fossil shells from Tertiary deposits are especially abundant along the Caloosahatchee River and in the region of Lake Okeechobee. In spite of their countless ages in a buried state, they are still so perfectly preserved that it is possible to determine that they show direct ancestral relation to present Floridan molluscan forms.

Geographically speaking, shells have a universal distribution. Within each geographic region are species characteristic of the region's various depths and temperatures. For example, only species adapted to cold waters will be found north of Newfoundland while the somewhat warmer shore waters south of Cape Cod encourage the development of moderate temperature species and the still warmer tropical waters from southern Florida to South America are extremely favorable for the development of tropical species in abundance.

A shell collector in the Florida region is greatly favored because there are not only the species characteristic of the different depths and temperatures of Florida waters but also an overlapping of these species with the species of other regions; for instance, the Transatlantic province somewhat overlaps the Caribbean province. The latter province includes Florida, the Bahamas, the West Indies, Florida Keys and the Gulf of Mexico. Such an extensive region is naturally very rich in molluscan genera and species which are adapted to specific areas, but, a collector should not expect to find all genera represented in a given locality. For example, forms found in the west coast Tampa Bay area would most likely not be included among those found in the region of the Florida Keys or the Fort Pierce area.

Shells have had a varied and world-wide use among races since the earliest known times. Early Mediterranean races used large shells as food and water receptacles. American Indians used the aristocratic cowries and tooth shells as money and objects of ornamentation. The well known cameos are carved from a species of helmet shell the structure of which is especially adapted to that art. A rich and costly purple dye was procured from the Muricidae in ancient times for coloring regal robes. Beautiful ornamental buttons are made from the pearly lining of certain clams. The regular symmetry and artistic sculpturing of the scallop shells has repeatedly inspired decorative designers; the oriental races are particularly clever at adapting shell motifs to decorative designs. Today in Florida shops are found many artistic and unique novelties, and souvenirs fashioned from shells which delight the tourists and shell enthusiasts.

A systematic classification of scientific material such as shell information is important. It avoids confusion in regard to the relationship of the numerous and varied species which an amateur collector is sure to encounter, and it is the only satisfactory way of presenting such material. The scientific groupings into which the animal kingdom is divided may at first seem confusing; but as soon as a few elementary facts are learned, comprehension of the systematic arrangement progresses rapidly.

The animal kingdom is first divided into two primary groups: the vertebrates or organisms with a backbone and the invertebrates or organisms without a back bone. Each of these groups is further divided into phyla. Each phylum is subdivided into classes, orders, families, genera, and species on the basis of variations in anatomical structure.

The phylum Mollusca belongs to the invertebrate group, and it includes all those organisms with a fleshy body which is surrounded by an outer muscular skin or mantle. A mollusk's mantle fold (with some exceptions) secrets a protective shell of calcareous composition. Complexity of structure places the phylum Mollusca high on the scale of invertebrate animals, and it is second on the scale of invertebrates as regards number of species.

The Mollusca are divided into five classes: Amphineura, Pelecypoda, Scaphopoda, Gasteropoda, Cephalopoda. In all classes except the Amphineura, the foot modifications provide the basis for class divisions. Representatives of all five classes are found in Florida waters, and a detailed description of them is given in this book in systematic order. Variations within the classes are numerous; therefore further dvisions into orders, families, genera and species is necessary. Two characteristics, however, are held in common by all mollusks—a mantle and a foot. Whenever live specimens can be obtained, a careful study of these features will prove interesting and instructive.

The binomial system of scientific naming has been consistently used because it has international understanding. Common names have too limited a regional meaning to be given general use. According to this system all genera and species names are of Latin or Greek or Latinized forms of words from other languages. For example, a species name is written thus, *Strombus pugilis* Linné. *Strombus* is the generic name, *pugilis* is the distinctive species name and Linné is the name of the author who originally defined and established the species. Species variations which have appeared repeatedly enough in different regions to be given sub-specific distinction are given a third name between the species name and the author's name, for example, *Strombus pugilis alatus* Gmelin. Charles W. Johnson's "List of Marine Mollusca of the Atlantic Coast from Labrador to Texas" (published in 1934) has provided the chief basis for the scientific arrangement, classification and nomenclature.

Molluscan shells have many interesting features the knowledge of which makes the comprehension of shells and collecting of shells more intelligible. With few exceptions, all mollusks have some form of shell which is present from the time or very shortly after the time the animal emerges from the egg capsule. Shell material is promptly added to this shell nucleus; this means that growth has already started. Shell growth is accomplished, and sculpture and color developed by secretions from the mantle's edge. Any unevenness in this edge results in characteristic shell sculpturing; and deformities in the edge due to injury result in altered sculpturing and patterning. Sculpturing also reveals the alternating growth and rest periods of mollusks. On univalves, axial ridges of varying prominence indicate growth periods; on bivalves, concentric ridges parallel to the margins indicate growth periods. Young shells do not have the finished form, sculpture, color, and pattern of mature shells; consequently the younger forms of some species differ considerably from the mature forms. Univalve animals are attached to their shells near the apex by means of a single strong muscle; bivalves are attached by one or two strong muscles at opposite ends on either valve. Shell color is thought to be very much controlled by light since the most brilliantly colored shells are found in shallow water and the upper valve of most fixed bivalves is more colorful than the lower valve.

The food and eating habits of mollusks vary widely. Microscopic organisms sucked in through the siphon constitute the food supply of pelecypods. Gasteropods with siphons are usually carnivorous; those without siphons are generally herbivorous. Gasteropods with a well developed radula bore through the shells of other mollusks, usually bivalves, and feed upon the tender animal within. For this reason the Oyster Drill, *Urosalpinx cinereus,* has become a great menace to oyster beds; and in some sections it has destroyed the oyster industry.

All mollusks either lay eggs or after laying their eggs retain them within their shells until the young are ready to hatch. Each species has its particular way of protecting its eggs from destruction and injury. Some form of tough capsule is usually constructed and these are strung together in various ways. By means of this structure, thousands of eggs can be deposited and protected at one spawning season. Pelecypod eggs remain within the parent shell until they are mature enough to be deposited.

The age limits of various molluscan species vary greatly. Some oysters are known to live from five to fifteen years while other mollusks live for only one year. The enormous size of some East Indian species indicates as many as seventy years of growth. The fact is that very little authentic knowledge of shell ages has been recorded.

It can now be concluded that a true shell enthusiast will be thrilled with the variety of interesting collecting possibilities within and near the Florida shores. The smaller, less colorful specimens will be no less interesting than the larger, fantastic and more colorful specimens. Each individual species can tingle the observer with the infinite beauty of the universe and the Divine control of order and creation.

Class: AMPHINEURA

There are five great classes of the phylum Mollusca. The distinctive bilateral symmetry of *Amphineura* (both sides of the nervous system similarly arranged) is what divides them into a class by themselves instead of the foot which is the basis of division for the other four classes. *Amphineura* are further divided into two orders (*Aplacophora*—having no plates, and *Polyplacophora*—having plates). The former order is represented by a very primitive molluscan form, and is almost never encountered upon beaches. The latter order is represented in Florida waters by several species.

The shell of the *Polyplacophora* or chitons consists of eight overlapping plates or valves which cover only the dorsal surface of the animal. These plates are held together by a tough girdle which completely surrounds the plates. Minute dots are scattered over the surface of some species which serve as sense organs or eyes. On the unprotected ventral surface is the muscular foot which is used for crawling and attachment to corals, rocks, and shells on which the chitons find their vegetable food. Chitons may be found clinging to hard objects brought up by high tide water.

Family ISCHNOCHITONIDAE

SLENDER CHITONS

Genus **ISCHNOCHITON** Gray 1847

Pimpled Chiton Ischnochiton papillosus A. B. Adams

COLOR: Exterior drab, variegated green; interior white.

SIZE: Length, about 8 mm.

RANGE: Florida west coast—Marco to Florida Keys.

DESCRIPTION: Shell small, sides slope slightly from mid-rib; side areas indefinitely shaped; girdle equipped with fine scales; small papillae uniformly cover the surface. This is the smallest of the Florida chitons.

FIG. A

BIVALVES
Class: **PELECYPODA**

The *Pelecypoda* make-up a very important class of the Mollusca both as to quantity of individuals and variety of structure. As compared to the *Gasteropoda* (the largest class of the phylum Mollusca) they have fewer genera and species but a greater number of individuals. To the class *Pelecypoda* belong the clams, scallops, oysters, mussels, and cockles. The common name "bivalve" is perfectly correct since all of the pelecypod animals have two valves or shells. Florida beaches, particularly along the Gulf Coast, are scattered and sometimes covered with thousands of strikingly beautiful bivalves which have been brought in by wind and wave.

A few explanations of the pelecypod animal anatomy will help the shell collector to understand many things pertaining to the structure and appearance of pelecypod shells. The mantle is a thin fleshy tissue which adheres, except for the free outer margin, to the inside of each valve, and it completely envelopes the animal at the two sides and back. Within its two halves or lobes are enclosed the essential organs—intestine, heart, gills, mouth, etc. Siphons or simple tubes are formed at the posterior end by the alteration of the mantle edges in this region. Through one of these tubes, water containing nutritive material passes into the body cavity where food material is removed; through the other tube, waste products and water are expelled. The foot, a muscular organ adapted for locomotion and burrowing, varies greatly with the different genera. In many genera this organ is equipped with a gland which secretes thread-like fibers forming a byssus which is used to attach the animal to some object. A head and eyes are absent from pelecypods. In a few instances eye-like structures are present on the mantle's edge and respond rapidly to light changes. Anatomical features form the basis for dividing Mollusca into classes, orders and sub-orders; therefore some knowledge of them should be helpful to the shell collector in organizing a collection systematically.

Shell features, however, provide the basis for classifying all species and some genera; so a knowledge of a few general facts about pelecypod shells should be an advantage to those interested in shells. In fact, with a reasonable amount of experience, one should be able to place a shell in its scientific family and genus at a glance. The two valves are held securely together along the dorsal margin by a tough ligament and interlocking teeth. The animals adductor muscles, the hinge ligament, and the elastic-like cartilage pad just below the hinge, control the opening and closing of the valves.

Each valve has an apex or umbone which usually points forward and is usually anterior to the hinge ligament. The umbones in most cases touch or nearly touch; but where the hinge margin is wide, the umbones are far apart. If the umbones are centrally located along the dorsal margin, the shell is said to be equilateral; if the umbones are nearer one end than the other, the shell is said to be inequilateral.

Shells whose valves are alike or nearly alike in size and shape are said to be equivalve. *Pecten gibbus* and *Venus mercenaria* are examples of this. Shells whose valves are not alike in size and shape are said to be inequivalve, for example,*Chama macerophylla* and *Anomia simplex*.

Bivalve measurements are usually determined as follows:

Length by measuring the greatest distance between the anterior and posterior margins.

Height or altitude by measuring the greatest distance between the umbones and the ventral margin.

There are four distinct margins to the shell. The dorsal margin has the hinge and umbones, the ventral margin is opposite the umbones, the anterior margin is the front edge, and the posterior margin is the back edge.

If a pelecypod shell is held with the ventral margin down, the hinge ligament toward the observer and the umbones directed away from the observer, the right valve will be on the observer's right and the left valve on the observer's left. This is the simplest way to distinguish between right and left valves.

The teeth of pelecypod shells, when present, are quite varied. The interlocking type has the cardinals in the center and the laterals on either side. If a row of comb-like teeth is present, there is no distinction between cardinals and laterals. The purpose of the teeth is to straighten the hinge mechanism and hold the valves more securely together.

The hinge ligament is a tough strip along the dorsal margin posterior to the umbones. This is usually external, and is very prominent in certain genera such as *Venus* and *Tellina*. In some genera there is a small platform, "the fossette," just below the cardinal teeth and inside the shell which bears the inner elastic portion of the ligament (Plate V, Fig. 8).

The accompanying diagrams together with the glossary definitions make clear additional parts of the pelecypod shell—particularly the inner surface markings.

The external surface of bivalves is most varied. Sculpture and ornamentation range from plain and smooth to deeply ribbed and highly noded or spined, and the color varieties and patterns are a marvel of combination and creation.

DIAGRAMS OF PELECYPOD SHELLS

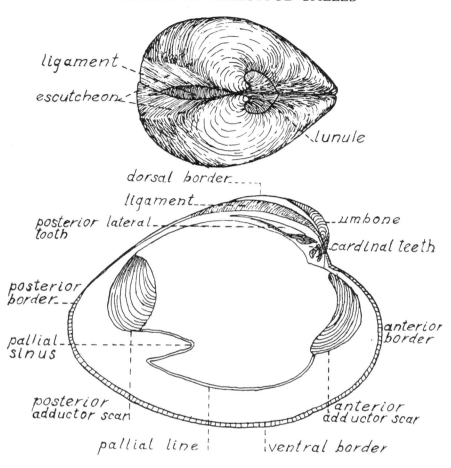

ligament

escutcheon

lunule

dorsal border

ligament

posterior lateral tooth

umbone

cardinal teeth

posterior border

pallial sinus

anterior border

posterior adductor scar

anterior adductor scar

pallial line

ventral border

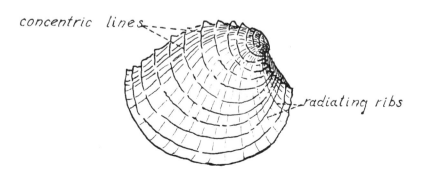

concentric lines

radiating ribs

ARK SHELLS
Family ARCIDAE

Species of this family are numerous, widely distributed, and adapted to a variety of Gulf Coast stations. Fossil remains of this family are frequently found; therefore the family must be of ancient origin.

Mollusks of this family demonstrate a keen sensitivity to light this serves primarily as a protective device against predatory sea species. When shadows pass or approach them, they quickly close their valves—an act of self-defense.

Arca shells are thick, either equivalve or inequivalve, coarsely ribbed, and covered with a thick, shaggy epidermis. The prominent umbones are widely separated by a flat angularly lined area. Characteristic comb-like teeth mark the length of the hinge margin of each valve.

Genus ARCA Linné 1758

Transverse Ark   Plate 1, Figure 1   Arca transversa Say

COLOR: White; epidermis, brown.

SIZE: Length, 1-1.5 inches.

RANGE: Florida east and west coasts.

DESCRIPTION: Shell rhomboidal, thick; valves nearly equal in size and shape; umbones prominent, widely separated; surface deeply marked with about thirty-five radiating ribs. This is a comparatively small Florida Ark shell.

Cut-rib Ark   Plate 1, Figure 2   Arca secticosta Reeve.

COLOR: White tinged with yellow, especially around the umbonal region; epidermis brown and shaggy.

SIZE: Length, 2-3.5 inches.

RANGE: Florida west and southwest coasts.

DESCRIPTION: Shell large, thick, equivalve, inequilateral; umbones anteriorly twisted, far apart; anterior and ventral margins curved, posterior margin angled, dorsal or hinge margin perfectly straight and equipped with fine comb-like teeth; many coarse radial ribs which are crossed about midway on valves by a coarse groove which ends at the posterior slope; interior marked with numerous fine striae; edge of margins coarsely toothed; muscle scars and pallial line distinctly marked.

Turkey's Wing   Plate 1, Figure 3   Arca occidentalis Philippi

COLOR: White ground with brown angular or zigzag markings; interior tinged with lavender; deeper lavender bordering margin; epidermis shaggy and tan.

SIZE: Length, 1.5-3 inches.

RANGE: Florida west and south coasts and as far north as St. Augustine in the east.

DESCRIPTION: Shell oblong, thick, equivalve, and inequilateral; umbones placed anterior to center, widely separated, and curved over hinge margin; anterior and ventral margins curved; posterior margin angled; hinge margin straight; area on either side of hinge margin flat; byssal notch in ventral margin below umbones; surface sculptured with strong radial ribs and fine interspacial threads; hinge of the family type.

Genus **NOETIA** Gray, 1847

Ponderous Ark   Plate I, Figures 4a, b   Noetia ponderosa Say

COLOR: Shell white inside and out; epidermis black and thick.

SIZE: Length, 2-2.5 inches.

RANGE: Florida west coasts; southern Florida coasts; Florida east coast.

DESCRIPTION: Shell extremely thick, equivalve, inequilateral; umbones prominent, curved inward, and far apart; anterior and ventral margins smoothly rounded; posterior margin obliquely slanted down from hinge area; hinge margin straight; radiating ribs are strong and about thirty-two in number; marginal crenulations are formed by termination of radial ribs; interior porcelaneous, smooth; muscular scars and pallial line deep. This species is very abundant on the Florida west coast from Tampa Bay to Sanibel Island.

SEA PEN SHELLS

Family **PINNIDAE**

In warm, moderately deep, Gulf Coast waters one can expect to find species of Pinnidae half buried in the bottom of the sea. The animal spins a long, silky, thready byssus by which the mollusk is anchored to subsurface stones and rocks.

Pinnidae shells are large, triangular-shaped, fragile, and translucent. The apex is sharp and anteriorly arranged. The posterior margin is rounded and slightly gaped; ventral margin curved; dorsal margin nearly straight and grooved to accommodate the elongated ligament. The shell interior has an irridescent lining covering slightly more than half of the surface. At certain times of the year shells of this family are extremely abundant on Florida west coast beaches.

Genus ATRINA Gray, 1840

Stiff Pen Shell   Plate I, Figure 5   Atrina rigida Dillwyn
Pinna muricata (of authors)

COLOR: Exterior, drab, translucent brown; part of interior, iridescent.

SIZE: Length, 6-10 inches.

RANGE: Florida Gulf coast.

DESCRIPTION: Shell has all the conspicuous family characteristics—thin, translucent, wedge-shaped; hinge margin straight; posterior margin rounded; ventral margin curved; radial ribs equipped with elevated tubular scales. These shells are abundant on the Florida west coast beaches.

Saw-Toothed Pen Shell   Plate I, Figure 6   Atrina serrata Sowerby
Pinna seminuda (of authors)

This shell also has all the conspicuous characteristics of the family Pinnidae. It is similar to the Stiff Pen Shell in size, shape, and color. The Saw-Toothed Pen Shell differs chiefly from the Stiff Pen Shell in the possession of shorter, more numerous scales which are arranged in closer-set radiating ridges.

PEARL OYSTER AND WING SHELLS
Family PTERIIDAE

To this family belong the distinguished "pearl oysters" of southern seas. A nacreous interior is a characteristic feature of all members of the family, particularly the native Floridan species.

The shells of this family are both inequivalve and inequilateral. The right valve has an opening for the accommodation of the byssus.

Genus PTERIA Scopoli, 1777
Avicula atlantica Lam. (of authors)

Atlantic Wing Shell   Plate I, Figure 7   Pteria columbus Roeding

COLOR: Exterior drab brown with fine, white, radiating, featherlike lines; interior iridescent, and nacreous.

SIZE: Length, 2-3 inches.

RANGE: Florida Gulf coast.

DESCRIPTION: Shell winged, eared, swollen, and obliquely extended toward posterior; inequivalve; hinge margain straight with posterior ear short or lengthened into wing-like structure; epidermis gives a scaly, rough appearance to the surface.

Genus PINCTADA Roeding, 1798

Pearly Oyster   Plate I, Figures 8a, b   Pinctada radiata Lamarck

COLOR: Exterior dull, reddish-brown; interior pearly with wide brown marginal border.

SIZE: Length, 1.5-3 inches.

RANGE: Florida east coast; Florida Keys; Tarpon Springs region on Florida west coast.

DESCRIPTION: Shell thin, compressed, eared—posterior ear not extended beyond posterior margin; exterior surface built up of thin plaits on which concentrically arranged scaly projections are sometimes developed. This is a curious shell and a fine addition to any collection.

Genus PEDALION Solander 1770

Winged-Tree Oyster.   Plate I, Figure 9   Pedalion alata Gmelin.

COLOR: Exterior drab tan or slate color; interior deep nacreous purple.

SIZE: Height about 3 inches.

RANGE: Florida Keys to West Indies.

DESCRIPTION: Shell much flattened. irregularly ovate; hinge margin straight and toothed with coarse, regularly arranged teeth with graduated lengths—longest ones at anterior end; right valve nearly flat; left valve slightly convex; outer surface decorated with flaky scales. Groups of P. alata are sometimes found attached to mangrove roots or other objects in shallow water.

OYSTER SHELLS

Family OSTREIDAE

Oysters have been known to be a food of man since primitive times. In our own country today the oyster culture industry nets millions of dollars annually. The edible Florida oyster is small but well flavored, and it is known to form large bars of considerable commercial importance in the shallow bay waters of the Florida west coast.

Shells of these marine species are very irregularly shaped and inequivalve. The left and larger valve remains fixed throughout its life to some substantial object. Other shell characteristics are obscure umbones, an internal hinge ligament, and a smooth, non-nacreous interior.

Genus OSTREA Linné 1758

Virginia or Common Oyster   Plate I, Figure 10   Ostrea virginica Gmelin

COLOR: Exterior dingy gray; interior dull white with reddish-brown spot near center.

SIZE: Length, 3-4 inches.

RANGE: Quiet shore and bay waters all around Florida coast.

DESCRIPTION: Shell thick, very irregularly elongated; inequivalve—upper valve smaller and flatter, lower left valve deep and fixed to some object at umbones; hinge has long depression for ligament; surface very rough, wrinkled and irregularly sculptured; size varies greatly. This is the most common of all the Florida oyster species.

Bush or Crested Oyster   Ostrea spreta d'Orbigny (O. cristata Born)
Plate I, Figure 11

COLOR: Drab brown or reddish-purple.

SIZE: Length 2-3 inches.

RANGE: Florida Gulf coast.

DESCRIPTION: Shell thick, inequivalve; shape irregular: margins coarsely serrate; attached umbone is longer than free umbone; surface rough and wrinkled. This species is plentiful in the region of mangroves in bays and quiet inside waters. It is an edible species but not delicious.

SPINY OYSTER SHELLS
Family SPONDYLIDAE

Extraordinarily clear coloring and unusual spiny processes make the "spiny oyster" a remarkable type of sea shell. Very fine specimens are often securely set in coral reefs in the Gulf of Mexico.

Spiny oyster shells are attached by the larger or right valve to hard sea bottom. Their strong hinge has a unique arrangement of two teeth which allow only partial opening of the valves.

Genus SPONDYLUS Linné 1758

American Thorny Oyster   Spondylus americanus Hermann
Plate I, Figure 12

COLOR: Great variety of vivid colors — red, yellow, orange, white, purple, and brown; interior white with a clearly marked, bright colored margin corresponding to the color of the exterior.

SIZE: Length, 3-5 inches.

RANGE: Florida east coast and southern Florida Keys.

DESCRIPTION: This shell shows characteristics of the family. Attached valve is less colorful and larger; free valve shows more distinct sculpturing of a radial spiny type. This is a remarkable and extraordinary sea shell.

Genus **PLICATULA** Lamarck 1801 (Plaited Shells)

Kitten's Paw   Plate I, Figures 13a, b   Plicatula gibbosa Lamarck

COLOR: Dull gray, tan, or white ground with rust colored hair-like lines or patches.

SIZE: Length, 20-25 mm.

RANGE: Florida east coast; Florida Gulf coast.

DESCRIPTION: Shell flat, thick, irregularly paw-shaped; surface sculptured with radial folds; terminations of folds produce coarsely crenulated margin.

SCALLOP SHELLS

Family PECTINIDAE

Species of Pectinidae are much sought after by shell collectors; in fact, some people specialize in making complete collections of nothing but pecten shells. Such a collection would be large for there are about two hundred and fifty species.

The animal is free swimming, lively, and capable of moving itself rapidly through the water by quickly opening and closing the valves. Well developed eyes are arranged along the fringed mantle edge which shows when the valves are somewhat open.

The shell surface is radially ribbed and the margins characteristically scalloped. The umbones are situated in the center of the straight hinge margin, the ears are equal or nearly so, and the shell is either equivalve or inequivalve.

Genus **PECTEN** Osbeck 1765

Fan Shell   Plate I, Figure 14   Pecten ziczac Linné

COLOR: Flat upper valve reddish-violet around ears and umbone, gray and reddish-brown stripes radiating from mid area to outer edges: lower convex valve tinted with a concentric arrangement of yellow, pink, and fawn colored bands; pale pink about umbone and ears.

SIZE: Length, 2 inches; width, 2 inches.

RANGE: Florida Gulf waters in from 3-5 fathoms of water.

DESCRIPTION: Shell scallop-shaped, inequivalve; ears not quite equal; flat upper valve slightly concave and sculptured with flat, radial ribs; concave lower valve sculptured with more rounded radial ribs.

Rough Scallop   Pecten muscosus Wood (P. exasperatus Sowerby)

Plate I, Figures 15a, b, c

COLOR: Uniform coloring on both valves; colors range from clear lemon yellow and pure orange to rich red and bright brown; interior colored with a tint of exterior color.

SIZE: Height, 30-45 mm.

RANGE: Florida coasts and Keys.

DESCRIPTION: Shell rough, moderately thick, nearly equivalve; ears unequal; margins evenly scalloped by terminations of ribs; regular radial ribs sculptured with fine, erect spines; interspaces minutely sculptured with bead-like radial ribs.

Yellow specimens are most rare. It is a thrilling experience to find these beautifully colored pectens. Strong storms often bring them to the beaches, and shallow tidal pools often harbor them.

Calico Shell   Plate III, Figures 1a, b, c   Pecten gibbus Linné

COLOR: A variety of mottled color patterns are produced by the combination of white with red-violet, reddish-brown, pinks, and purples. The lower valve is not so brightly colored; in some instances, it is white with tinges of the upper valve coloring around umbone.

SIZE: Height, 20-40 mm.

RANGE: Florida Gulf coast.

DESCRIPTION: Shell exhibits usual Pecten characteristics; nearly equivalve; rounded radial ribs; terminations of ribs form characteristically scalloped margin. At some seasons this is one of the most abundant beach specimens.

Many-Ribbed Scallop   Pecten gibbus irradians Lamarck

Plate III, Figures 2a, b, c, d, e

COLOR: Variable; upper valve has variegated pattern of

brown, grey, and white; lower valve white with brown umbonal area. Variegated patterns of yellow or orange are not so common.

SIZE: Height, 1.5-3 inches.

RANGE: Florida west coast bay waters.

DESCRIPTION: Shell shows all the salient characteristics of the family Pectinidae. The radial ribs and interspaces are crossed by minute thread-like, concentric lines.

Lion's Paw or Knobby Scallop   Plate III, Figure 3   Pecten nodosus Linné

COLOR: Dark red or burnt orange.

SIZE: 3 to 4 inches high and wide.

RANGE: Florida, south of Jupiter Inlet on the east and Tampa Bay on the west.

DESCRIPTION: Shell characteristically scallop-shaped but ornately sculptured. Radial sculpture consists of heavy ribs and wide interspaces. Ribs are sculptured with ridges and curious elevated nodes which are concentrically arranged; interspaces are also sculptured with fine ridges; ears and lateral edges are more coarsely ridged. Concentric sculpturing consists of fine lines which are sometimes equipped with minute scales in interspaces. Interior is ribbed and channeled to correspond with exterior sculpturing. This is an unusually ornate bivalve and rather rare. It is sometimes dredged in 4-6 fathoms of water around rocky bottom. An observing collector can expect to find occasional ones on the beaches after a hard blow—especially a northwest blow.

FILE SHELLS

Family LIMIDAE

Members of this family are adapted to a variety of depths in all seas. The animals have an elaborately constructed mantle which, in living mollusks, is interesting to observe and beautiful to see.

The shells of the family Limidae are equivalve and eared. The umbones are rather far apart. The anterior margin is straight and the posterior margin is rounded.

Genus LIMA Roeding 1798

Rough File Shell   Plate II, Figure 1   Lima inflata Lamarck

COLOR: Alabaster white; epidermis, brown.

SIZE: Height, 1-3 inches.

RANGE: Florida, south of Jupiter Inlet on the east and south of Cedar Keys on the west.

DESCRIPTION: Shell thin, translucent, inequilateral,, and ob-liquely-ovate; eared with anterior ear recurved; umbones sharp and small; surface sculptured with irregular radiating ridges which are equipped with file-like scales from mid area to margin; concentric growth lines interrupt the radial ridges.

JINGLE SHELLS
Family ANOMIIDAE

Young mollusks of this family are free swimming, but the adults are fixed to other shells or solid sea objects by means of a byssus which extends through a small opening or notch in the lower or left valve.

The shells have a slightly nacreous surface and are semi-trans-parent.   They are abundant on the Florida west coast beaches.

Genus ANOMIA Linné 1758
Baby's Foot Print or Jingle Shell   Anomia simplex d'Orbigny
Plate II, Figures 2a, b, c, d

COLOR: Lustrous yellow, orange, slate, cream, or white.

SIZE: Height, 20-50 mm.

RANGE: Florida, south of Jupiter Inlet on the east and south of Cedar Keys on the west.

DESCRIPTION: Shell thin, translucent, inequivalve; shape ir-regular and determined by outline of object to which it is fixed; lower valve flat with byssal perforation at apex; upper valve con-vex with muscle scar shaped to suggest a baby's foot print. This species is extremely abundant on the Florida west coast beaches. A handful of these, when rattled, gives a jingling sound; hence they are given the common name, "Jingle shell."

MUSSEL SHELLS
Family: MYTILIDAE

The family Mytilidae has an extensive geographic distribution and its many species inhabit either open or inside waters.

The shells are equivalve, and extremely inequilateral. The great-est length is from the acute umbones to the opposite border. The long hinge ligament is marginal and internal.

Genus MYTILUS Linné 1758

Hooked Mussel   Plate II, Figure 3   Mytilus recurvus Rafinesque

COLOR: Somber purple ground; whitish ribs, nacreous purple interior with pale polished lavender marginal border.

SIZE: Length, 1-1.5 inches.

RANGE: Florida east and west coasts, especially in shallow inside waters.

DESCRIPTION: Shell moderately thick, sharply curved; umbones pointed and placed at anterior end; margin serrate; surface sculptured with a divided or branched type of radial rib; growth lines are concentric and distinct.

Scorched Mussel   Plate II, Figure 4   Mytilus exustus Linné

COLOR: Greyish-lavender and brown with brown epidermis; interior nacreous purple with pale nacreous lavender border.

SIZE: Length, 20-30 mm.

RANGE: Florida west and southwest coast.

DESCRIPTION: Shell fragile, obliquely-elongated, and swollen in region below hinge margin; surface strongly striate with regularly arranged striae which are crossed by conspicuous concentric ridges. This is an abundant Florida west coast shell and is often found high up on the beaches among sea weed and debris after high tide.

Genus MODIOLUS Lamarck 1799

Tulip Horse Mussel   Plate II, Figures 5a, b, c   Modiolus tulipus Linné

COLOR: Pearly foundation overlaid with a layer of either lavender, pink, or light brown; interior iridescent; epidermis dark brown.

SIZE: Length, 1-2 inches.

RANGE: Florida Gulf coast.

DESCRIPTION: Shell obliquely-elongate, inflated, fragile, and translucent; umbones anteriorly placed, curved inward, and nearlv touching; surface roughened by incremental lines.

CYRENA SHELLS

Family CYRENIDAE

The Cyrenidae are abundant in brackish-water. The shell is roughly ovate and equipped with both lateral and cardinal teeth.

Genus **POLYMESODA** Rafinesque 1820 (Cyrena of authors)

Sarasota Anthus   Polimesoda floridana sarasotaensis Henderson
Plate II, Figures 6a, b

COLOR: Concentrically arranged streaks of purple and cream color; deep purple escutcheon; interior deep purple.

SIZE: Length, 30 mm.

RANGE: Tampa Bay area.

DESCRIPTION: Shell roughly oval, thin; umbones nearly touching; surface marked with minute concentric lines; three cardinal and two lateral teeth; posterior end eroded. This brackish-water specimen is often found in bayous.

CARDITA SHELLS
Family **CARDITIDAE**

The Carditidae endure a variety of temperatures at medium depth. Their shells are equivalve, robust, and ribbed.

Genus **CARDITA** Bruguiere 1792

Broad-ribbed Cardita   Plate II, Figures 7a, b   Cardita floridana Conrad

COLOR: Fresh specimens are dull bluish-purple or reddish-brown; beach-worn specimens show white ground with spots of superimposed reddish-brown; interior, porcelaneous white.

SIZE: Length, 1 inch.

RANGE: Florida Gulf coast.

DESCRIPTION: Shell obliquely-elongate, thick, equivalve, inequilateral; umbones small, conspicuously curved inward; lunule small, impressed; surface sculptured with fifteen to eighteen heavy, obtusely scaled, radiating ribs and fine concentric growth lines; marginal terminations of ribs produce a coarsely scalloped margin. This is a rather abundant west coast bay species.

ROCK OYSTER SHELLS
Family **CHAMIDAE**

Shells of this family are inequivalve, solid, and fixed by either the right or left valve. The fixed valve is larger and more rounded than the free valve. The hinge ligament is external and strong.

Genus **CHAMA** Linné 1758

Leafy Rock Oyster   Plate III, Figure 4   Chama macerophylla Gmelin

COLOR: Various shades and tints of pink, yellow, white, and purple; interior white.

SIZE: Length, 1.5 inches.

RANGE: Florida east coast; Florida west coast from Tampa Bay to Marco Island.

DESCRIPTION: Shell thick, irregularly rounded, inequivalve; lower valve deep and fixed; upper valve free and flat; umbones twisted; surface sculptured with well developed foliations with fluted edges; internal margin finely lined.

Genus ECHINOCHAMA Fischer 1887

Chest Rock Oyster Plate III, Figures 5a, b Echinochama arcinella Linné

COLOR: White with rust-colored stains in umbonal area; interior white with purple posterior and ventral area.

SIZE: Height, 30-50 mm.

RANGE: Florida west coast.

DESCRIPTION: Shell thick, inflated; valves and umbones have a forward twist; lunule distinctly outlined and deeply impressed; surface sculptured with eight or nine coarse, spine-bearing ribs; interspaces, lateral areas, and lunule are papillaceous. Unique sculpturing distinguishes this shell.

LUCINA SHELLS
Family LUCINIDAE

Some members of the family Lucinidae are plentiful along the Florida west coast from the Sarasota region to Cape Romano. The animal's foot is long and conveniently constructed for digging.

Lucinidae shells are equivalve, and roundish. The umbones are depressed, small, and directed forward.

Genus LUCINA Bruguiere 1797

Pennsylvania Lucina Plate III, Figure 6 Lucina pennsylvanica Linné

COLOR: Pure white; epidermis, light brown.

SIZE: Width, 2 inches.

RANGE: Florida east coast.

DESCRIPTION: Shell extremely thick, rounded inflated; umbones small, depressed, pointed, and curved forward; lunule deeply outlined; raised, concentric folds produce a ridged surface—especially in region of margins.

Thick Buttercup Plate III, Figure 7 Lucina pectinata Gmelin
Jamaica Lucina Lucina jamaicensis Lamarck

COLOR: White diffused with yellow ;interior white with yellow margin.

SIZE: Width, 2 inches.

RANGE: Florida east coast south of St. Augustine; Florida west coast south of Cedar Keys.

DESCRIPTION: Shell rounded, moderately thick, rather com pressed; umbones flat and close; the depressed line running obliquely from the umbones to the posterior-ventral margin is a characteristic feature; outer margins smooth; sculpture consists of raised concentric ridges.

Florida Lucina   Plate III, Figure 8   Lucina floridana Conrad

COLOR: Pure white.

SIZE: Width, 35 mm.

RANGE: Florida west coast.

DESCRIPTION: Shell moderately thick, much compressed, rounded; umbones very small, pointed, and curved forward; surface smooth except for fine growth lines.

Woven Lucina   Plate III, Figures 9a, b   Lucina nassula Conrad

COLOR: Shell, white inside and out.

SIZE: Height 13 mm.; length, 11 mm.

RANGE: Florida east and west coasts.

DESCRIPTION: Shell small, rounded, equivalve, nearly equilateral; umbones nearly touch; lunule distinct; surface delicately and distinctly sculptured with erect, concentric lines and numerous fine, radial ribs which produce a woven-like or reticulated surface; both cardinal and lateral teeth are present; pallial line and muscle scars distinct. This shell is often found in shallow water.

Genus CODAKIA Scopoli 1777

Tiger Lucina   Plate III, Figure 10   Codakia orbicularis Linné

COLOR: Pure white or white tinged with yellow or red-violet around the edges.

SIZE: Width, 3 inches.

RANGE: Florida Gulf coast and Florida Keys.

DESCRIPTION: Shell large, moderately thick, and orbicular; umbones very small and depressed; surface reticulated by crossing of fine radiating ribs and distinct but fine concentric growth lines. This species favors sandy bottom; and it is the largest of the Florida Lucinas.

Genus **LORIPINUS** Monterosato 1883

Golden-Mouthed Lucina   Loripinus chrysostoma Philippi

Plate III, Figures 11a, b

COLOR: Exterior white; interior bright, orange, especially from the mid area to the margins.

SIZE: Width, 40-50 mm.

RANGE: Florida Gulf coast.

DESCRIPTION: Shell thin but strong, translucent, very inflated and most orbicular of the Florida Lucinas; hinge ligament weak; surface marked by fine concentric striae. The golden interior of this shell is very striking.

COCKLE SHELLS

Family **CARDIIDAE**

Mollusks of the family Cardiidae are characterized by having two prominent siphons and an abruptly angled foot.

Cardiidae shells are equivalve. The sculpture varies from smooth to coarsely ribbed. Margins are crenulate. Sizes and shapes vary but all exhibit a heart-shaped end view. The teeth are characteristically curved.

Genus **CARDIUM** Linné 1758

Rose Cockle   Plate III, Figure 12   Cardium isocardia Linné

COLOR: Exterior color consists of a mottled arrangement of tan and white with a tinge of violet around the umbones; interior intensely colored with hues of violet and salmon; anterior area white.

SIZE: Height, 1-2 inches

RANGE: Florida west coast, especially from Tampa Bay to Cape Sable.

DESCRIPTION: Shell cordate, thick; umbones rounded and prominent; margins deeply crenulated; teeth arranged as in C. *magnum;* surface ornamented with heavy radiating ribs which are equipped with erect spiny processes or scales. This is an exceptionally colorful cockle shell.

Yellow Cockle   Plate III, Figures 13a, b   Cardium muricatum Linné

DESCRIPTION: This shell is similar in size, shape, range, and surface decoration to the Rose Cockle (*C. isocardia.*) Color differences are noted in the greater amount of reddish-brown and yellow in the mottled pattern of the exterior; and within, a clear yellow band follows the margin and a pale yellow tint is diffused over most of the interior.

Large or Brown Cockle   Cardium robustum Solander
Plate III, Figure 14

COLOR: Color pattern of buff, yellowish-brown and reddish-brown disposed into irregular bands of color; posterior slope brown or purplish-brown; interior has shades of chestnut brown with an arc of white around anterior margin.

SIZE: As large as 5 inches high and 4 inches wide.

RANGE: Florida west coast from Clearwater to Cape Sable.

DESCRIPTION: Shell large, thick, strikingly cordate; valves swollen; posterior margin obliquely lengthened; umbones large and prominent; hinge ligament strong; ventral margin conspicuously crenulated; surface sculptured with thirty-three to thirty-seven rounded radial ribs. This is the largest of the Florida Cockles.

Genus **PAPYRIDEA** Swainson, 1840
Spiny Paper Cockle   Plate III, Figure 15   Papyridea spinosum Meuschen

COLOR: Fine mottled arrangement of cream color and reddish-purple, a solid reddish-purple area often surrounds the umbonal area and ventral margin of the shell; interior white with exterior colors showing through.

SIZE: Length 35-40 mm.

RANGE: Florida south of Jupiter Inlet in the east and as far north as Cedar Keys in the west.

DESCRIPTION: Shell lengthened transversely, thin, gaping at both ends; surface sculptured with obliquely radiating, slightly spinose ribs—most conspicuous spines on posterior portion of shell; shell inequilateral; umbones nearer anterior end; margins finely serrate.

Egg Cockle   Laevicardium serratum laevigatum Lamarck
Plate III, Figure 16

COLOR: Polished ivory color with a tinge of orange around the margin and umbones.

SIZE: Height, 1-2 inches.

RANGE: Florida east coast.

DESCRIPTION: Shell smooth, polished, inflated; margins minutely serrate. The smooth texture and thinness of this shell remind one of an egg shell.

Genus **LAEVICARDIUM** Swainson, 1840
Large Egg Cockle   Plate III, Figure 17   Laevicardium serratum Linné

COLOR: Cream color with zigzag or wavy concentric markings of light brown; interior polished white sometimes tinged with pink.

SIZE: Height, 2-3 inches.

RANGE: Florida west coast.

DESCRIPTION: Shell inflated, strong, cordate, posterior margin obliquely elongated; umbones high; posterior slope distinctly set off from remainder of valve by having a smooth, nearly straight surface; exterior smooth but faintly ribbed especially near ventral margin; interior margin thickened and faintly toothed. This shell is abundant on the west coast, especially in the Tampa Bay area.

VENUS SHELLS
Family **VENERIDAE**

Exquisite shape, color, and pattern give the family Veneridae a select place in the class Pelecypoda. In addition to artistic distinction, they have distinction of quantity and size. For there are more genera and species in the Venus family than any other family of pelecypods. The species range in size from very small to very large.

The shells are equivalve, robust, and elegantly rounded or elongated. Three cardinal teeth are divergent and the lateral teeth vary considerably in size and shape. The interior surface is polished and porcelaneous.

Elegant Dosinia   Piate IV, Figure 1   Dosinia elegans Conrad

COLOR: White with straw-colored epidermis.

SIZE: Length, 2-3 inches.

RANGE: Florida west coast, especially from Tampa Bay to Sanibel Island.

DESCRIPTION: Shell rounded compressed; umbones high and pointed forward; lunule small, cordate, well impressed; ventral margin subcircular; cardinal teeth placed on an elongated fossette; pallial sinus very deep and acutely angled; surface sculptured with regular, comparatively wide, concentric ridges. This is a very charming little Florida west coast sea shell.

Genus DOSINIA Scopoli, 1777

Disk Dosinia   Plate IV, Figure 2   Dosinia discus Reeve

COLOR: Dull white, usually with some cream-colored concentric bands; epidermis straw-colored.

SIZE: Length, 2-3.5 inches; width, the same.

RANGE: Florida east coast, especially in the locality of St. Augustine.

DESCRIPTION: This shell retains all the genus characteristics of *Dosinia elegans* but it is more disk-shaped, more compressed and the concentric ridges are finer and flatter. *Dosinia discus* is rarer than *Dosinia elegans*.

Spotted Clam   Plate IV, Figure 3   Macrocallista maculata Linné

COLOR: Light pinkish-fawn ground with brown spots more or less stroked in as if with a flat edged brush; two radial bands of brown spots extend from the umbones to the ventral margin; shellac-like epidermis persists around the lower edges and tends to darken the pattern in this area; interior white tinged with violet in central area.

RANGE: Florida west coast, wide distribution.

SIZE: Length, 2-3 inches; height, 1.5-2 inches.

DESCRIPTION: Shell subovate, strong, smooth; umbones high and twisted forward; lunule indefinitely defined; margins smooth; pallial sinus obliquely truncate.

Genus MACROCALLISTA Meek, 1876

Sun-Ray Shell   Plate IV, Figure 4   Macrocallista nimbosa Solander

COLOR: Light pinkish-fawn ground with darker pinkish-fawn, slightly curved radial streaks; epidermis dull grey.

SIZE: Length, 4-5 inches.

RANGE: Florida west coast especially from Sarasota to Marco Island.

DESCRIPTION: Shell elongate-oval, thick, equivalve; hinge ligament somewhat immersed; lunule elongated, moderately impressed; pallial sinus deep and obliquely truncated; surface smooth; color rays broken or interrupted by plain concentric ridges. This is an exceptionally graceful and beautifully decorated Florida shell.

Genus CHIONE Megerle von Mühlfeld, 1811

Cross-Barred Venus   Plate IV, Figure 5a, b   Chione cancellata Linné

COLOR: Dull white sometimes streaked with light brown; interior purple, medium brown or white.

SIZE: Length, 1 inch

RANGE: Florida east coast; Florida west coast, especially from Tampa Bay to Sanibel Island.

DESCRIPTION: Shell thick, roughly triangular, equivalve, and inequilateral; lunule distinctly defined; escutcheon distinctly set off from dorsal margin; posterior margin longer than anterior margin; ventral margin rounded; surface sculptured with thin, erect, concentric ridges which cross flatter, more numerous, radiating ribs and produce a characteristic cancellated surface. This is a very abundant Venus shell in the Tampa Bay to Sarasota area.

Genus VENUS Linné, 1758

Hard-Shelled Clam   Plate XII, Figures 1a, b   Venus mercenaria Linné

COLOR: Drab grayish-white; interior pure white or white with violet border around muscle-scars and ventral margin.

SIZE: Width, 3-5 inches.

RANGE: Extensive range; entire Florida east coast; southern coast; Florida Gulf coast.

DESCRIPTION: Shell large, very thick, equivalve, and inequilateral; umbones rounded, and turned forward; lunule small, cordate, and distinctly defined; escutcheon clearly set off; ligament strong, and external; adductor muscle-scars deep; pallial line and sinus distinct; numerous fine lamellar ridges ornament the surface. This is a very common edible clam which is good eating if not too old and tough.

Genus ANOMALOCARDIA Schumacher, 1817

Thick-Shelled Heart   Anomalocardia cuneimeris Conrad
Plate IV, Figures 6a, b

COLOR: Variable—white, shades of fawn and brown, pale green, and zigzag brown patterns on pale ground color; interior white and brown or white and purple.

SIZE: Length, 20 mm.

RANGE: Florida as far south as Lake Worth in the east and Sanibel Island in the west.

DESCRIPTION: Shell small, very inflated, posterior end much extended; lunule moderately distinct, escutcheon flat; umbones close together; surface sculptured with deep grooves and rounded ridges which are especially prominent in anterior area and inflated mid area.

TELLIN SHELLS

Family TELLINIDAE

Many species of the Tellinidae are so splendidly colored and delicately sculptured that they are rated as aristocratic bivalves.

The combination of an exceptionally slender siphon and a forceful foot make it possible for the animal to burrow deep into the sand.

Shells of the Tellinidae are compressed, have the anterior end rounded, and the posterior end somewhat pointed and folded. The umbones are small and very close together. The ligament is strong and external.

Members of this family are numerous and distributed in all seas.

Genus TELLINA Linné, 17

Lined Tellin   Plate IV, Figures 7a, b   Tellina lineata Turton

COLOR: Pink or white. Pink variety is deep pink in umbonal area fading out to pale pink or white at margins; interior polished iridescent pink. White variety is white inside and out but a fine, faint, pink line comes down obliquely from the umbone in the front on each valve; epidermis, pale brown.

SIZE: **Length 30 mm.**

RANGE: Florida east and west coasts.

DESCRIPTION: Shell small, thin, translucent, compressed umbones very small; posterior portion reflected to the right; posterior margin nearly straight; anterior and ventral margins rounded; minute, close-set, compressed, concentric lines are engraved on the surface.

Alternate Tellin   Plate IV, Figures 8a, b, c   Tellina alternata Turton

COLOR: Polished white and pale yellow or white and delicate pink; interior highly polished pale yellow or pale salmon-pink.

SIZE: **Length, 2 inches.**

RANGE: Florida Gulf coast.

DESCRIPTION: Shell compressed smooth; umbones acute but small, slightly posterior to center; ligament external; anterior end rounded; posterior end angled, folded and slightly reflected to right; exterior sculptured with wide, compressed, concentric ridges —each alternate ridge is lost on the flattened posterior portion.

Great Tellin   Plate IV, Figure 9   Tellina magna Spengler

COLOR: Right or upper valve delicately rayed with pale orange, deep orange on umbone. Left or lower valve white or white with faint yellow rays, deep orange on umbone. Interior polished white with a diffused patch of orange beneath the umbone on each valve.

SIZE: Length, 3-4 inches.

RANGE: Florida—Santa Rosa Island in northwest Florida and Palm Beach region in southeast Florida.

DESCRIPTION: Shell large, thin, smooth, polished and compressed; umbones small and posterior to center of shell; ligament immersed; posterior fold distinct; anterior and ventral margins rounded; posterior part of shell pointed and reflected to right; edges sharp and thin; surface sculptured with numerous, minute compressed, concentric lines. This is the largest of the Florida Tellinas.

Sunrise Tellin   Plate IV, Figure 10   Tellina radiata Linné

COLOR: Polished white with pale yellow from umbones to mid area; broad rose colored rays extend from umbones to margins; interior white with external color showing through.

SIZE: Length, 2-3 inches.

RANGE: Florida east coast to Key West.

DESCRIPTION: Shell elongate, smooth, polished; ligament strong and external; anterior end rounded; ventral margin rather straight; posterior fold slight but posterior twist pronounced. This bivalve is noted for its striking coloration.

Var. of Sunrise Tellin   Tellina radiata unimaculata Lamarck
Plate IV, Figure 11

COLOR: The same as T. *radiata* except that rose colored rays are lacking; beaks rose colored.

SIZE: Length, 2-3 inches.

RANGE: Florida east coast to Key West.

DESCRIPTION: Shell the same as T. *radiata* except for the color variation.

Genus **TELLIDORA** Mörch, 1856
Crested Tellin   Plate IV, Figure 12   Tellidora christata Récluz

COLOR: Translucent, alabaster white.

SIZE: Length, 25 mm

RANGE: Florida west coast.

DESCRIPTION: Shell small, thin, extremely compressed—left valve flatter; umbones pointed; ligament weak; anterior margin arched; posterior margain straight; ventral margin well rounded;

fine, tooth-like projections ornament anterior and posterior edges; surface obtusely ridged; fine erect ridges near ventral margin. This is an exceptionally dainty little bivalve.

SEMELE SHELLS
Family SEMELIDAE

Mollusks of the family Semelidae bury themselves in muddy sand at moderate depths. By means of a powerful, painted foot and two relatively long, slender siphons they are able to live in such hidden homes.

Their shells are usually rounded, compressed, and slightly bent in the posterior end. The external ligament is short.

Genus SEMELE Schumacher, 1817

Beautiful Striped Semele   Semele bellastriata Conrad
Plate V, Figures 1a, 1b

COLOR: Yellowish-brown rayed with brownish-purple; interior polished brownish-purple.

SIZE: Length, 20 mm.

RANGE: Florida west coast to Key West.

DESCRIPTION: Shell small, oblong, substantial; surface beautifully sculptured with regularly arranged growth lines and distinct radiating ribs forming a reticulated surface.

Florida Semele   Plate V, Figure 2   Semele proficua Pulteney

COLOR: Chalky white to pale pink; epidermis light brown; interior white or white streaked with brownish purple or pink.

SIZE: Length, 25-30 mm.

RANGE: Florida west coast; Florida east coast from Palm Beach southward.

DESCRIPTION: Shell thin, rounded, somewhat inflated; both lunule and escutcheon are present but small; margins thin but strong; surface slightly roughened by fine concentric lines.

Purple Semele   Plate V, Figure 3   Semele purpurascens Gmelin

COLOR: Exterior delicate whitish-lavender or yellow with pale purple, zigzag, concentric pattern; interior polished with speckled purple pattern running from umbones to below middle area; margins pale purple or white.

SIZE: Length, 25-30 mm.

RANGE: Florida east and west coasts.

DESCRIPTION: Shell rounded translucent; umbones flat and pointed; surface sculptured with numerous fine concentric lines.

WEDGE SHELLS
Family DONACIDAE

The Donacidae live in the surface layer of wave washed beach sand where they can be collected in quantities at the proper season along the Florida west coast. It is interesting to observe the gayly colored creatures hastening to rebury themselves after each wave washes away the surface sand.

Genus DONAX Linné, 1758

Coquina or Variable Wedge Shell   Donax variabilis Say
Plate V, Figures 4a, b, c, d

COLOR: Variable and gay; all colors of the rainbow are found in these shells; rays and concentric lines of color are arranged so as to produce plaid and striped color patterns.

SIZE: Length, 20 mm.

RANGE: Florida east coast; southern Florida coast; Florida Gulf coast.

DESCRIPTION: Shell small, wedge-shaped, and equivalve; anterior end elongated; ligament external and strong, consequently valves are usually found on the beaches in pairs; surface sculptured with distinct radial ribs and concentric growth lines; margins finely toothed.

These little mollusks are unusually abundant on the Florida beaches in April. After the receding waves have washed the sand from them they can be seen by the hundreds quickly burrowing deeper into the moist sand before the next wave comes to expose them.

Family SANGUINOLARDIIDAE

In some respects these mollusks are related to the Semeles, and Tellinas because they burrow in sandy soil, have a strong foot, and long slender siphons.

Their shells are inequilateral, semitransparent, and usually finely sculptured.

Genus ASAPHIS Modeer, 1793

Cockle Clam   Asaphis deflorata Linné   A. coccinea **Martyn**

Plate V, Figure 5

COLOR: Exterior color ranges from pale yellow to orange, rose pink and violet—deeper color around umbonal region; interior color corresponds with exterior but is more intense and uniformly distributed; a deep purple streak is usually found on posterior margin of interior.

SIZE: Length, 1.5-3 inches.

RANGE: Southeast Florida to West Indies.

DESCRIPTION: Shell obliquely elongated, equivalve; and translucent; umbones small and close together; hinge ligament external; surface sculptured with numerous, distinct, wavy, radial ribs which are crossed by distinct, concentric, growth lines which are more conspicuous near the margins.

This is a strikingly sculptured and colored shell. It is occasionally taken on the east coast but its main centers of distribution are the Bahamas and West Indies.

RAZOR CLAM SHELLS

Family SOLENIDAE

The shells of the Solenidae are equivalve and so much elongated that they are given the common name, "razor clam."

The animal is edible but difficult to capture because of its rapid burrowing habit.

Genus SOLEN Linné, 1758

Green Razor Clam   Plate V, Figure 6   Solen viridis **Say**

COLOR: Pale green and white with crescent-shaped brown marks across the mid area of the shell; epidermis, greenish-brown.

SIZE: Length, 2 inches.

RANGE: Florida, south of St. Augustine in the east and as far north as Cedar Keys in the west.

DESCRIPTION: Shell long, narrow, fragile; hinge margin nearly straight; ventral margin slightly curved; surface and margins smooth.

BEACH OR SURF CLAM SHELLS
Family MACTRIDAE

The large family Mactridae has universal distribution, and is adapted to sandy shore waters. The main distinguishing feature of the shell is the "fossette" or cartilage plate just under the umbones on which the internal ligament rests. In the region of the umbones, the valves are rather swollen. The shells are equivalve and elongated transversely. The muscle scars, pallial line, and pallial sinus are well marked.

Genus MACTRA Linné, 1767

Frail Clam　　　Plate V, Figure 7　　　*Mactra fragilis* Gmelin

COLOR:　　Polished white with straw-colored or light brown epidermis.

SIZE:　　Length, 2-2.5 inches.

RANGE:　　Florida, south of St Augustine in the east and as far north as Cedar Keys in the west.

DESCRIPTION:　　Shell shows characteristics of the family. Shell thin, elongate; anterior and posterior margins are slanting; posterior portion bent and gaping; margins sharp; very fine, compressed concentric sculpturing.

Genus SPISULA Gray, 1838

Plate V, Figure 8
Solid Surf Clam　　　*Spisula solidissima similis* Dillwyn

COLOR:　　Chalky white with straw-colored epidermis

SIZE:　　Length, 2-4 inches.

RANGE:　　Florida, south of St. Augustine in the east and as far north as Cedar Keys in the west.

DESCRIPTION:　　Shell thick, elongate; hinge ligament weak; lateral teeth long and thin; pallial line clear; pallial sinus not deep; fossette or cartilage plate just inside and under the umbones is the most distinguishing feature. Every collector will observe that this is the most abundant bivalve on the Florida west coast beaches. This is the southern variety of the northern *Spisula solidissima*.

Genus ANATINA Schumacher, 1817
Subgenus RAETA Gray, 1853

Sailor's Ear or Channeled Duck　　　*Anatina canaliculata* Say
Plate V, Figure 9

COLOR:　　Exterior pure white; interior glossy white.

SIZE:　　Length, 2-2.5 inches.

RANGE:　　Florida Gulf coast.

DESCRIPTION: Shell obliquely-oval, thin, inflated, and gaping posteriorly; surface sculptured with high ridges and wide deep interspaces or channels which are impressed through to interior.

ANGEL WING SHELLS
Family PHOLADIDAE

Mollusks of the family Pholadidae are excavators. They burrow into wood or soft rock and keep enlarging this lodging-place by rotating the shell and scraping away the surface with the anterior end of the valves.

Shells of this family are equivalve, white, thin, brittle, elongated transversely, and gaping at both ends. The posterior end is somewhat tapered. The inconspicuous umbones are made more so by the reflected, anterior end of the hinge margin. A long, blunt-ended, slightly curved, tooth-like structure projects from under the umbonal region.

Genus **BARNEA** (Leach) Risso, 1826

Angel's Wings   Plate IV, Figures 13a, b   Barnea costata Linné

COLOR: Pure chalky white.

SIZE: Length, 5 inches.

RANGE: Florida east coast in region of St. Augustine, Florida west coast to Marco Island.

DESCRIPTION: Shell thin, brittle, elongate, and inflated; umbones nearly covered by the reflected, anterior end of the hinge margin; tooth-like process projects from under umbonal region and curves toward center of valves; finely toothed, radial ribs and distinctly engraved growth lines ornament the surface. This species burrows deep into sand, wood, or soft rock. The shell's wing-like contour and exquisite sculpturing account for the common name of "Angel's Wings."

Truncated Angel's Wings   Plate IV, Figure 14   Barnea truncata Say

COLOR: Translucent, chalky white.

SIZE: Length, 40-60 mm.

RANGE: Southwest Florida to Florida Keys

DESCRIPTION: Shell oblong, thin; valves twisted; umbonal region flat and curved; anterior end pointed; posterior end truncate; surface sculptured with fine ribs and distinct concentric growth lines especially about margins. This is a delicate shell which lives around the roots of mangrove trees in shallow water.

TOOTH SHELLS
Class: SCAPHOPODA

Mollusks of this class have a pointed foot much resembling the prow of a boat; hence they are given the name *Scaphopoda*. It is the smallest class of the phylum. Anatomically, the animal differs so greatly from other mollusks of the phylum that it was not classified as a mollusk until the first quarter of the nineteenth century. This classification, however, is based on the fact that the animal has a mantle, foot, and radula.

Its rank is between the *Pelecypoda* and *Gasteropoda*. It resembles the former in having a pointed foot and symmetrical organization; and no head and tentacles. The single shell unit and radula relate it to the *Gasteropoda*. Fine contractible filaments on either side of the mouth serve as breathing organs and food catchers. Reproduction takes place by means of the unisexual method.

They are considered degenerate molluscan animals because they do not have the highly organized respiratory and circulatory systems with gills and a heart which are characteristic of mollusks in general.

The shells are tubular, slightly curved, and open at both ends. Since the growing region is the anterior or largest end, the greatest tapering is at the posterior end.

This is a curious shell—very much resembling an elephant's tusk; and it is truly in a class by itself. Certain Indian tribes collected quantities of these shells for ornamental and mercenary purposes until a more practical medium of exchange was established.

Family DENTALIIDAE

The Dentaliidae have a deep water range and bury themselves in the miry sea bottom. Through the larger, deeply buried, anterior end of the shell the animal's foot and filaments project in search of food; the siphon projects from the smaller, posterior end which is obliquely angled with the surface.

The Dentaliidae shells are white, elongated, tubular-shaped structures which are open at both ends. The surface is usually simply sculptured and possessed of either a chalky or a polished texture.

Panelled Tooth Shell   Dentalium laqueatum Verrill

COLOR: White.

SIZE: Length, 45 mm.

RANGE: Sandy regions of Florida Keys, close to Gulf Stream.

DESCRIPTION: Aperture fluted circle; tip pronouncedly curved; sculpture consists of nine to twelve prominent ribs and concave intercostal areas which become less prominent near anterior end.

FIG. B

UNIVALVES
Class: GASTEROPODA

The class *Gasteropoda* is the largest class of the phylum Mollusca and it includes the greatest number of genera and species. All the characteristic molluscan traits are present in this class although some of them show much modification. Conchs, cowries, whelks, and periwinkles are among its members. The three distinctive class features are:

1. Asymmetry—the animal cannot be divided by a median longitudinal line into similar halves.

2. The head is a distinct organ and in most species is well developed.

3. The shell is spirally arranged and of one unit.

The animal itself is well developed. When living and extended out of the shell, it carries the shell in a horizontal position; that is, the notch or canal is anterior, the apex is posterior, and the aperture is downward. The siphon, when present, is anteriorially placed and is used for sucking water into the gills. It may be short, long, or lacking. In the latter case, a fold in the anterior part of the mantle serves as a siphon. The gasteropod head is distinct; and tentacles, when present, project from the sides of the head. Eyes are usually mounted midway between the top and bottom of the tentacles. A narrow slit on the front portion of the head serves as the mouth. The mantle-edge may be short and not project beyond the edge of the shell, or it may be very large and when extended may enclose most of the shell as in the cowries (*Cypraea*). The gasteropod foot is broad, flat, elongated, and greatly varied. It so closely resembles a stomach when crawling that the name *Gasteropoda*—meaning "stomach-foot"—has been given to this class of the phylum. Coiled within the throat of the univalve is the radula—a ribbon-like, fleshy-strip equipped with rows of teeth upon one side. This is a most important organ since it is used for boring into other shells and tearing out fleshy food. A special horny development, the operculum, on the dorsal side of the foot serves to close the aperture when the foot is retracted.

Several forms of reproduction are found among the gasteropods; some are hermaphroditic, some are unisexual, and some are viviparous. Egg capsules, varying in form with the genera, are the usual structures provided for depositing the spawn.

Since the gasteropod shell consists of a single unit, it is called an "univalve." Simply speaking, its shape may be described as a cone spirally arranged about a central column. Such modifications of this cone as high or low top, thick or thin middle, and flat or extended base, result in the infinite variety of univalve shells.

After a trip to the beach, the amateur collector should lay out the assortment of univalve shells and note the wide variety of their general character. It will be observed, for example, that some shells are elongated, have many whorls, and small apertures; others are short, have few whorls, and large round apertures. Sorting a collection according to prominent conchological features is the first step in shell classification.

To go further with classification and identification, a knowledge of the essential parts of a gasteropod shell is necessary. The accompanying diagrams together with the following explanations should prove helpful to a studious collector. To examine an univalve shell, hold it with the apex up and the aperture facing the observer. At the extreme top of the shell is the apex. Below this are several whorls of graduated sizes. All except the last and largest whorl compose the spire. The interstices between each whorl are called sutures. They vary in depth from very shallow to very deep. The last and largest whorl is the body-whorl in which is found the aperture or mouth. The shape of the mouth varies from nearly round to long and narrow. Through this opening the animal extends the foot and other extendible parts. The outer edge of the aperture or mouth is called the outer lip. This shows wide variation throughout the class gasteropoda. The inner lip or columella may be plain or marked with folds. This columella or central column extends the full length of the shell and serves as an axis for the revolving whorls. The anterior notch, when present, varies greatly and may be extended into a closed or simi-closed canal. The posterior notch, when present, is at the upper end of the aperture and is for the disposal of the anal discharges. An umbilicus, or hollow pit extending from the center of the base into the body-whorl, is evident in some shells. A good example of this is the Cat's Eye, *Polinices duplicata*. This shows that the gasteropod shell is whorled about an imaginary axis.

Gasteropod shells are either dextral (having whorls turned to the right) or sinistral (having the whorls turned to the left). In the former arrangement the opening is on the right. Most marine species are of this type. The sinistral type has the opening on the left, and is exemplified by the Left Handed Whelk, *Busycon perversum*.

The surfaces of gasteropod shells are so variously sculptured, ornamented, colored, and patterned that word descriptions of them are inadequate. The interested collector will need nothing more than his own eyes to show him the marvelous varieties in shell surfaces; and through continued study and observation come increased interest in and appreciation for these incredible creations of nature.

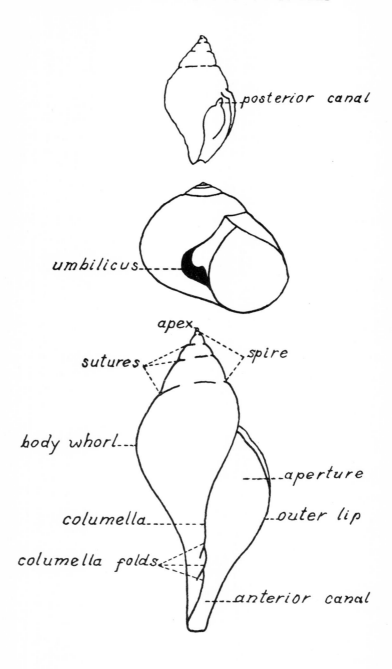

KEYHOLE LIMPETS AND LITTLE CHINK SHELLS
Family FISSURELLIDAE

This extensive family, commonly called the keyhole-limpet family, is adapted to a wide range of depth. The animals are vegetarian and free swimming. A large foot, brief snout, and tentacles equipped with eyes are distinctive anatomical features.

The shells have low conical shapes, and are broadly ovate beneath. An apical perforation or anterior margin notch or slit serves for the elimination of excretions. The exterior surface is sculptured with radial ribs which terminate in either a smooth or crenulate margin. Smoothness characterizes the interior.

Genus FISSURELLA Bruguiere, 1791

Barbados Chink   Plate VI, Figure 1   Fissurella barbadensis Gmelin

COLOR: Dull white, grey or green; fine reddish-purple lines between smaller ribs; patches of purple or brown between and on the bolder ribs; interior wall has alternating bands of green and white; interior callus around opening, green with brownish edge.

SIZE: Length, 20-35 mm.

RANGE: Florida Keys, south Florida coast, up to the east coast as far as St. Augustine.

DESCRIPTION: Shell conical, thick, moderately elevated; anterior and posterior slopes nearly straight; apex subcentral and perforated by a nearly round orifice; sculpture consists of many radiating ribs, eleven of which are heavier and extend from the orifice; all eleven are evenly spaced except the two which are close together at the anterior median line; margin coarsely crenulate.

Genus LUCAPINA Gray, 1857

Cancellated Lucapina   Lucapina cancellata Sowerby
Plate VI, Figure 2

COLOR: White, grey or dull green; interior white with dark or blackish perforation callus.

SIZE: About 20 mm. long.

RANGE: Florida Keys and West Indies.

DESCRIPTION: Shell oblong and conical; apex anterior to center; aperture oval and slightly truncate behind; sculpture consists of alternating large and small, radiating ribs crossed by conspicuous concentric ridges. Intersection of ridges and ribs are nodular.

Genus DIADORA Gray, 1821

Keyhole Limpet   Plate VI, Figure 3   Diadora alternata Say

COLOR: Greyish-white or drab yellow.

SIZE: Length, 22 mm.

RANGE: Florida east and west coasts.

DESCRIPTION: Shell oblong, conical; peak anterior to center; anterior side slightly concave; posterior side slightly convex; aperture keyhole-shaped; lattice-like sculpturing produced by three small ribs between two larger ribs being crossed by fine regular concentric lines; interior callus around aperture thick, and truncate, with depression abruptly posterior; margin finely crenulate.

TOP SHELLS

Family TROCHIDAE

This large family of mollusks has many genera and species which are, for the most part, stationed in the littoral region of warm tropical seas. The Pacific and Indian oceans have beautiful pearly species.

The herbivorous animals have a short snout, two tenacles on the head, and several cerri on either side of the foot which are very active when the animal is in motion. The operculum has a central nucleus and is corneous.

Shells of the family Trochidae vary greatly in size and shape, but the typical form is top-shaped. The base is flat, the whorls are compact, and the apex is acute. The beautiful nacreous interior of the aperture is a persistent family feature.

Genus LIVONA Gray, 1842

West Indian Top-Shell   Plate VI, Figure 4   Livona pica Linné

COLOR: Wavy or zigzag streaks of black on a pale green to white background; interior pearly and iridescent.

SIZE: Length, 3-4 inches.

RANGE: Florida Keys, occasionally as far north as Charlotte Harbor on the west coast.

DESCRIPTION: Shell top-shaped, large, thick; sutures wavy or irregular; aperture subcircular; outer lip sharp-edged and somewhat thickened just within; umbilicus deep, round and possessed of a tooth-like callus; outer surface corrugated by irregular sculpturing. This species is common throughout the West Indies but it

- 56 -

is questionable whether living specimens of the species have been taken in Florida waters. Dead specimens have been found on the Florida west coast in the region of Charlotte Harbor.

Genus CALLIOSTOMA Swainson, 1840

Florida Top-Shell   Calliostoma jujubinum perspectivum Philippi
Plate VI, Figure 5

COLOR: Buff ground with reddish-brown streaks of color more or less axially disposed; iridescent, white interior.

SIZE: Length, 15 mm.; width of base, 15 mm.

RANGE: Florida west coast from Cedar Keys south to Cape Sable.

DESCRIPTION: Shell typically top-shaped; apex acute; base flattened; sutures rather indistinct; umbilicus conspicuous and funnel-shaped; outer lip simple; aperture angled at basal margin; fine bead-like spiral ribs ornament the surface.

TURBAN AND STAR SHELLS

Family TURBINIDAE

Some features of this family resemble those of the family Troch-idae but the calcareous, externally convex operculum is definitely different.

Their shells are turbinate and have rounded or oval apertures. Beneath the layer of surface sculpture is a pretty pearly layer which often shows if the surface layer is chipped.

Genus TURBO Linné, 1758

Knobby Top   Plate VI, Figures 6a, b   Turbo castaneus Gmelin

COLOR: Orange, fawn or gray often marked with alternating streaks of light and dark color corresponding to the ground color; interior of aperture, pearly.

SIZE: Length, 25-30 mm.

RANGE: Florida west coast from Tampa Bay southward to the Florida Keys.

DESCRIPTION: Shell turbinate, strong; whorls five to six and rounded; aperture subcircular; outer lip crenulated; columella thickly callused; surface sculptured with highly beaded spiral lines alternating with finely beaded striae in interstices.

Genus **ASTRAEA** Roeding, 1798

Long-spined Star Shell   Plate VI, Figure 7   Astraea longispina Lamarck

COLOR: Exterior white or greenish-brown; interior white and polished.

SIZE: Diameter of base, 35-60 mm.

RANGE: Florida Keys and West Indies.

DESCRIPTION: Shell thin, depressed; base flat; spines elongated, flattened, and projected over the sutures; umbilicus often open and conspicuous but shell is usually imperforate.

Short-spined Star Shell   Astraea brevispina Lamarck
                              Plate VI, Figure 8

COLOR: White or dull yellow-orange.

SIZE: Diameter of base, 40 mm.

RANGE: Florida Keys and West Indies.

DESCRIPTION: Shell moderately thin; base flat; circumference acutely keeled; spines short, flat and projected slightly beyond the sutures; additional sculpturing knobby and spirally arranged; umbilicus open and conspicuous; area around umbilicus reddish-orange.

American Star Shell   Plate VI, Figure 9   Astraea americana Gmelin

COLOR: Dull white or greyish.

SIZE: Diameter and length, about 1 inch.

RANGE: Florida Keys and West Indies.

DESCRIPTION: Shell robust, elevated; whorls sculptured with oblique, radial folds; aperture obliquely-oval; outer lip usually crenulate.

Carved Star Shell   Plate VI, Figure 10   Astraea caelata Gmelin

COLOR: Drab buff or green.

SIZE: Diameter, 2 inches.

RANGE: Florida Keys and West Indies.

DESCRIPTION: Shell solid, pyramid-shaped; aperture obliquely oval, and large; outer lip sharp and crenulated; umbilicus imperforate; base flattened and sculptured with radial striae and several coarse concentric ridges; whorls ornamented with semitubular spiny processes.

SEA SNAIL SHELLS
Family NERITIDAE

The Neritidae are found almost exclusively in warmer tropical sea waters. The animals have a short snout and long tenacles, are herbivorous, and deposit their eggs on their own shells and the shells of other animals.

The extremely inflated body whorl, flattened spire, and semi-circular aperture combine to give the shell a peculiar subcircular shape. The calcareous operculum is shaped to fit the characteristic tooth-like projections on the columellar margin.

Genus NERITA

Bleeding Tooth   Plate VII, Figures 1a, b, c   Nerita peleronta Linné

COLOR: Variable; body-whorl usually shows streaks and patches of purple on a white, pale orange, or greyish-yellow ground; spire usually of a plain ground color; outer lip porcelaneous white; columellar margin stained with patches of red-orange.

SIZE: Diameter, 1-1.5 inches.

RANGE: Florida Keys to the West Indies.

DESCRIPTION: Shell obliquely-ovate; body-whorl ventricose; spire depressed; apex acute; outer lip sharp-edged but thickened within; sculpture consists of flat, evenly spaced spiral ridges; operculum shaped to fit the irregularly-shaped aperture with its tooth-like projections. This species prefers rocky stations and clings to solid objects and coral reefs.

Baby's Teeth   Plate VII, Figure 2   Nerita tessellata Gmelin

COLOR: White spiral ribs decorated with purple strips which form an irregular checkered pattern; ribs of spire often pale yellow; aperture porcelaneous white.

SIZE: Diameter, 15-20 mm.

RANGE: Florida Keys to West Indies.

DESCRIPTION: Shell obliquely-ovate, small, and solid; spire short; apex sharp; body-whorl relatively large; outer lip crenulated on edge, toothed within; columellar area flat and toothed in center.

MOON SHELLS
Family NATICIDAE

The animals in this family have a broad, oval foot which cannot be drawn entirely within the shell. When the animal is active, the fully extended foot hides nearly all of the shell. The sense of smell and touch in these animals seems well developed as is also the radula the structure with which the animal drills through bivalve shells in search of the succulent animal within.

The Naticidae shells are subglobular because of the inflated body whorl and depressed spire. The aperture is semilunar and the outer lip is simple.

Genus NATICA Scopoli, 1777

Little Moon Shell   Plate VII, Figure 3   Natica canrena Linné

COLOR: White ground; whorls decorated with chestnut colored bands of wavy lines, zigzag lines, and short dashes; shell base white; interior of aperture light chesnut fading into white at lip edge.

SIZE: Length, 1-1.5 inches.

RANGE: Florida Gulf coast, Florida Keys, and Florida east coast.

DESCRIPTION: Shell subglobular, smooth; body-whorl much expanded; spire short; aperture semilunar; outer lip sharp-edged; umbilicus conspicuous and partially covered with callus.

Shark's Eye   Plate VII, Figure 4   Natica maroccana Dillwyn

COLOR: Whorls diagonally streaked with strips of olive-grey, dull yellow, purple, and white; base white; callus partially covering umbilical area and wall of aperture dark brown.

SIZE: Diameter, about 40 mm.

RANGE: Florida southwest coast to West Indies.

DESCRIPTION: Shell thick, and elevated giving a turbinate contour; aperture oblong-ovate; outer lip thick and smooth; umbilicus large but partially covered by brown callus; operculum is distinguished by double marginal ridge—the outer ridge being more elevated than the inner; shell surface smooth but not polished.

Genus POLINICES Montfort, 1810

Milky Moon Shell   Plate VII, Figure 5   Polinices lactea Guilding

COLOR: Polished milky white.

SIZE: Length, 18-25 mm.

RANGE: Southern Florida coast and up the east coast to Palm Beach area.

DESCRIPTION: Shell thin, subglobular; spire much depressed; apex sharp; sutures distinct; body-whorl very ventricose; aperture semi-circular; outer lip thin and sharp; umbilicus partially covered by white reflected callus; surface smooth, porcelaneous and marked with minute growth lines.

Cat's Eye   Plate VII, Figure 6   Polinices duplicata Say

COLOR: Light bluish or ashy white on whorls, creamy white on base; umbilical callus and interior of aperture, chestnut colored.

SIZE: Length, 1-2 inches.

RANGE: Florida Gulf coast and Florida east coast as far north as St. Augustine.

DESCRIPTION: Shell thick, smooth, obliquely-ovate, and somewhat wider than high; spire short; body-whorl expanded; aperture semi-lunar; outer lip simple and curved to meet the body-whorl at an acute angle; umbilicus conspicuous and partially covered by a thick callus.

Genus SINUM Roeding, 1798

Flat Moon Shell or Ear Shell   Sinum perspectivum Say

Plate VII, Figure 7

COLOR   Creamy-white.

SIZE: Diameter of base, 30 mm.

RANGE: Florida east coast south of Jupiter Inlet; Florida west coast south of Clearwater.

DESCRIPTION: Shell translucent but strong, extremely depressed, and auriform; aperture widely flared; interior polished; sculpture consists of minute, slightly wavy, spiral grooves and striae crossed by fine growth lines.

CRUCIBLE SHELLS
Family CALYPTRAEIDAE

The mollusks of this family are firmly fixed throughout their life time to hard surfaces such as rocks or shells. The animal muscles are attached to a small, shelly, cup-shaped structure on the interior which gives a peculiar character to the shell.

Genus CRUCIBULUM Schumacher, 1817

Cup and Saucer Limpet Plate VII, Figure 8 Crucibulum striatum Say

COLOR: Greyish-white streaked with brown.

SIZE: Diameter of base, 25-30 mm.

RANGE: Florida southeast, south, and southwest coasts.

DESCRIPTION: Shell cone-shaped; apex curved to the side; surface marked with many fine radiating ribs; internal cup-shaped structure attached to one side. This species is often found clinging to hard sea objects somewhat below low-tide line.

SLIPPER SHELLS
Family CREPIDULIDAE

These widely distributed mollusks are fixed, in adult stages, to any convenient hard surface. The irregularly oval shells, though free, vary considerably in shape because they take on in young stages the form of the surface on which they rest. The spire is imperfect and the partial partition in the shell cavity is a conspicuous feature.

Boat Shell or Baby's Cradle   Crepidula fornicata Linné
Plate VII, Figures 9a, b

COLOR: White ground with curved, chestnut-colored stripes variously disposed; a band of brown often borders the white diaphragm; epidermis straw-colored.

SIZE: Length, 30 mm.

RANGE: Florida Gulf, south, and east coasts.

DESCRIPTION: Shell obliquely ovate; apex curved down to the margin of the shell and not distinct from the body-whorl which forms the main part of the shell; diaphragm covers approximately half of aperture, is thin and translucent.

Flat Slipper Shell   Plate VII, Figure 10   Crepidula plana Say

COLOR: White.

SIZE: Length, 30 mm.

RANGE: Florida Gulf coast and Florida east coast.

DESCRIPTION: Shell ovate, translucent, flat; apex pointed and terminal; diaphragm covers slightly less than half the length of the shell; exterior surface roughened by concentric growth lines; inner surface polished. The character of the shell curvature is determined by the shape of the object to which it is attached—large shells, rocks, or other hard sea objects.

Thorny Slipper Shell Plate VII, Figure 11 Crepidula aculeata Gmelin

COLOR: Exterior tan or brown; interior highly polished brown and white; diaphragm white.

SIZE: Length, 20-35 mm.

RANGE: Florida coasts to West Indies.

DESCRIPTION: Shell possesses general *Crepidula* characteristics; exterior sculptured with irregular, radiating, spiney ridges.

SUNDIAL SHELLS

Family ARCHITECTONICIDAE

Shells of the family Architectonicidae are substantial, very much flattened, and conspicuously umbilicated. The opening to the umbilicus is crenulated, and the base of the shell and shell whorls are delicately and precisely sculptured.

Genus ARCHITECTONICA Roeding, 1798

Granulated Sundial Shell   Architectonica granulata Lamarck

Plate VII, Figure 12

COLOR: Lavender and white with tan spots on ridge next to suture.

SIZE: Diameter, 1-1.5 inches.

RANGE: Florida east coast southward to southern Florida Keys.

DESCRIPTION: Shell thick, flattened, top-shaped; umblicus strongly crenulated; base flat and decorated with many coiled, granulated ridges; body and spiral whorls sculptured with furrows and ridges which are segmented into dots and dashes forming a pattern resembling a sun dial.

PERIWINKLE SHELLS

Family LITTORINIDAE

The Littorinidae are very well known as littoral region mollusks. Many of them live long periods above high tide mark.

The animal's foot shows unusual molluscan construction. A longitudinal split in the bottom of the foot divides it into two parts. These act alternately when the animal moves.

Genus LITTORINA Férussac, 1822

Lined periwinkle   Plate VII, Figure 13   Littorina irrorata Say

COLOR: Tannish-white with a greyish tinge about the apex; spiral ridges of spire faintly marked with brown lines; columellar callus glazed burnt-orange.

SIZE: Length, 20-30 mm.

RANGE: Florida, as far south as Charlotte Harbor on the west coast and Indian River on the east coast.

DESCRIPTION: Shell thick, elongated, cone-shaped; chalky shell quality; apex sharp; aperture ovate; outer lip sharp-edged, thickened within and curved to meet the body-whorl at an acute angle; surface sculptured with a spiral arrangement of flat ridges and engraved lines and grooves. This species also prefers brakish water inlets where it clings to piling, roots and grass stems.

Angulated Periwinkle Plate VII, Figure 14 Littorina angulifera Lemarck

COLOR: Cream colored ground; spirally arranged reddish-purple dashes decorate the fine ribs and produce a more or less distinct linear pattern.

RANGE: From southern Florida to St. Augustine in the east and Cedar Keys in the west.

DESCRIPTION: Shell cone-shaped, thin, translucent; body-whorl rounded; spire high and sharp; aperture ovate; outer lip thin; surface sculptured with fine spiral grooves and ridges. This periwinkle prefers salt water inlets where it is often found attached to mangrove roots and branches, piling, and wharves; thus it remains for long periods out of water.

Genus **TECTARIUS** Valenciennes, 1833

Spiny Periwinkle   Plate VII, Figure 15   Tectarius muricatus Linné

COLOR: Exterior light bluish-white with white tubercles; top of spire dull pink; columella and lip white; interior of aperture tan.

SIZE: Diameter, 15-20 mm.

RANGE: East Florida, west Florida, and Florida Keys.

DESCRIPTION: Shell solid; spire high; apex acute; aperture nearly circular; outer lip simple with inside indented opposite each beaded row; umbilicus elongated into a slit; nuclear whorls sculptured with thread-like spiral lines, other whorls sculptured with spirally arranged beaded rows. This species is commonly found well above high tide line in rocky regions.

TURRIT SHELLS
Family **TURRITELLIDAE**

The Turritellidae are widely distributed. Their shells have many whorls and the spire shows extreme tapering.

Genus **TURRITELLA** Lamarck, 1799

Variegated Screw Shell   Turritella variegata Linné
Plate VIII, Figure 1

COLOR: Marbleized pattern of reddish-brown on dark fawn ground.

SIZE: Length, 2-3 inches.

RANGE: Southeast Florida coast to West Indies.

DESCRIPTION: Shell turriculate, solid; spire high; apex acute; whorls fifteen to sixteen; sutures distinct and subchanneled; aperture subcircular; lip simple; surface sculptured with spiral ridges alternating with fine striae.

WORM SHELLS
Family VERMETIDAE

Members of this family have a curious worm-like appearance. The first coils of young shells are regularly arranged; but after this short growth is completed, pronounced irregularity develops. The general shape of the animal corresponds to the shape of the shell. The snout is short and the eyes are arranged on the outside of the short tentacles.

Shells of the Vermetidae are usually fixed. They have been found growing in sponges, in colonies of their own kind, and fixed to corals and rocks.

Genus VERMETUS Daudin, 1800

Irregular Worm Shell   Vermetus irregularis d'Orbigny

Plate VIII, Figure 2

COLOR: Light chestnut fading into white toward aperture.

SIZE: From a few inches to several feet long.

RANGE: Southwest Florida coast is deep water.

DESCRIPTION: These shells usually form big clumps or colonies. Individual shells irregularly coiled and twisted; nuclear tip is slightly more regularly coiled; aperture round; surface marked with a few clearly keeled, longitudinal ribs and many fine longitudinal lines, wrinkled growth lines encircle the coils.

Genus VERMICULARIA Lamarck, 1799

Worm Shell   Plate VIII, Figure 3   Vermicularia spirata Philippi

COLOR: Ashy-white merging into yellowish-brown toward aperture.

SIZE: Length, 6-10 inches.

RANGE: Florida west coast from Tampa Bay southward to southwest Florida Keys; Florida east coast from St. Augustine southward.

DESCRIPTION: Youngest whorls are regularly coiled, oldest whorls are loosely coiled; aperture circular; surface sculptured with coarse encircling growth lines, heavy longitudinal ribs and fine longitudinal lines. Individuals of this species often live together in masses or clumps.

Family MODULIDAE

The warm Floridian waters provide a favorable environment for three species of the family Modulidae.

Genus MODULUS Gray, 1842 and 1847

Florida Button   Modulus modulus floridanus Conrad
Plate VIII, Figure 4

COLOR: Light buff with small dark brown spots and patches.

SIZE: Diameter, 10-15 mm.

RANGE: Florida, as far south as Biscayne Bay in the east and as far south as Marco in the west.

DESCRIPTION: Shell small, strong, umbilicate; body-whorl comparatively large; spire depressed; outer lip thin; columella equipped with tooth-like fold at extreme end; base sculptured with spiral cords; shoulder sloping and sculptured with slightly nodose, axial ridges.

HORN SHELLS
Family CERITHIIDAE

Most of the Florida Cerithiidae live in the littoral zone and, are often found in shallow water among grasses or stones.

The animals can attach themselves to objects by means of secreted, thread-like structures.

Salient shell characters are: a long spire with many whorls, small aperture, and short anterior canal.

Genus CERITHIUM Bruguiere, 1789

Little Horn Shell   Cerithium algicolum C. B. Adams
Plate VIII, Figure 5

COLOR: White with blotched or thread-like brown markings in a spirally arranged pattern.

SIZE: Length, 20-30 mm.

RANGE: Southern Florida to West Indies.

DESCRIPTION: Shell solid, elongated; spire tapering, apex acute; sutures distinct; eight to ten whorls sculptured with a spiral beaded cord immediately below sutures and finer thread-like spiral lines on remaining part of whorls. These lines are crossed by long-itudinal ribs giving a nodular surface at intersections; aperture ovate; outer lip thin.

Brown Horn Shell   Plate VIII, Figure 6   Cerithium floridanum Mörch

COLOR: Ivory ground with brown spiral striations.

SIZE: Length, 40-50 mm.

RANGE: Chiefly Florida Gulf coast.

DESCRIPTION: Shell greatly elongated; spire high; apex acute; axial sculpturing consists of several nodose ribs which are interrupted by sutures and spiral sculpture; spiral sculpture consists of a coarse, nodose peripheral ridge and numerous fine revolving striae; aperture ovate; arterior canal short; varix opposite aperture.

Variable Cerithium   Cerithium variabile C. B. Adams
Plate VIII, Figure 7

COLOR: Dark brown speckled with white.

SIZE: Length, 10-13 mm.

RANGE: Florida east coast, Florida west coast, and Florida Keys.

DESCRIPTION: Shell solid, small; spire tapering; apex acute; aperture ovate; anterior canal short; outer lip finely crenulate; conspicuous varix opposite outer lip; body whorl sculptured with seven beaded spiral lines, succeeding whorls sculptured with three beaded spiral lines.

Small Cerithium   Plate VIII, Figure 8   Cerithium minimum Gmelin

COLOR: Color varies from jet black to black with white sutural band and ashy gray with white.

SIZE: Length, 10-13 mm.

RANGE: Florida west coast from Tampa Bay southward; Florida east coast from Lake Worth southward.

DESCRIPTION: Shell small, slender, tapering; aperture ovate; lip thin and simple; six whorls sculptured with irregular longitudinal ribs made nodulose by crossing spiral threads and coarser spiral ridges; anterior canal acutely reflected. Sheltered places between tide lines are abundant with these in the spring.

C. minimum nigrescens Menke—name given to the solid black type.

C. minimum septemstriatum Say—name given to the black type with white sutural band.

Fly-Specked Cerithium   Plate VIII, Figure 9   Cerithium muscarum Say

COLOR: Drab bluish-brown or reddish-brown ground with white nodes and brown specks on axial ribs.

SIZE: Length, 20-25 mm.

RANGE: Tampa Bay to southern Florida Keys.

DESCRIPTION: Shell tapered; apex sharp; sutures distinct; whorls convex; aperture oval; anterior canal short and recurved; strong varix opposite opening; nodose axial ribs interrupted at suture; spiral ridges and lines revolve about the whorls.   These shells are so abundant at certain times that they can be gathered in handfuls in sheltered, shallow water regions.

Genus **CERITHIDAE** Swainson, 1840

Ladder Shell   Plate VIII, Figure 10   Cerithidea scalariformis Say

COLOR: Light russet-brown spirally banded with dark brown and fawn color; axial ridges white.

SIZE: Length, 18-24 mm.

RANGE: Lower Florida east coast and Florida west coast from Cedar Keys southward.

DESCRIPTION: Shell thin, tapering, turriculate; sutures well marked; aperture nearly circular, interior of aperture polished; outer lip thickened, reflected and somewhat produced below; surface of the ten convex whorls sculptured with slightly curved, regularly placed, spirally arranged, vertical ribs. *Certithidea scalariformis* is frequently found climbing up the grasses on tidal salt flats.

CONCH OR STROMB SHELLS

Family **STROMBIDAE**

The Strombidae are fascinating mollusks.   The animals seem to be extra animated because they can jump and rotate the shell from side to side.   These actions are accomplished by means of a strong, narrow foot at the end of which is a claw-like operculum serving as a support.   Strong jaws and teeth, and a keen sense of sight and smell aid these mollusks greatly in their search for carrion food.

Their shells are strong and thick; the body-whorl elongated and large.   At the anterior end of the long aperture is a characteristic "stromb" notch.   The long outer lip is gracefully flared.

These mollusks prefer water depths ranging from low tide line to twelve fathoms.   Within this range their carrion feeding habits are sufficiently satisfied.

Genus STROMBUS Linné, 1758

Giant Conch Plate XII, Figure 2 Strombus gigas Linné

COLOR: Ground color buff finely lined with light brown; elegant pink on columellar area and interior of aperture; deep pink fading into pale pink or white on flared outer lip.

SIZE: Length, 6-12 inches.

RANGE: Southern Florida Keys and Key West.

DESCRIPTION: Shell large, strong; spire tapered; sutures indistinct; aperture long; stromboid notch only slightly developed; anterior canal short and recurved; outer lip flaring with upper end raised or produced; axial nodes on spire become increasingly larger as they approach the body-whorl where they culminate in spiny processes; spiral sculpture consists of coarse striae. This species favors sandy bottom but is also found on rocky bottom.

Fighting Conch Plate IX, Figures 1, 1a Strombus pugilis Linné

COLOR: Spire ivory with light brown streaks, body-whorl darker brown; interior color varies from salmon pink to lavender and deep purples; epidermis brown.

SIZE: Length, 3-4 inches.

RANGE: Florida west coast, especially in Sarasota region, and southward to Sanibel Island.

DESCRIPTION: Shell elongate; spire tapered; apex acute; body-whorl elongate and tapered toward base; sutures distinct; aperture long and narrow; outer lip thickened and wing-like; stromboid notch well developed; deep basal notch recurved; prominent nodes on shoulder of largest whorls; base of body-whorl marked with strong striations; columellar callus and interior of lip highly polished. The authors have collected dozens of fresh dead specimens of *S. pugilis* on the beaches in the region of Sarasota following severe Gulf storms.

Young Fighting Conch shells are commonly found on the Florida west coast. They are about one inch long, have tan and white color markings, and fine spiral lines.

Winged Stromb Plate IX, Figures 2, 2a Strombus pugilis alatus Gmelin

COLOR: Mixture of white and tan, or white and brown; a zigzag pattern of light and dark band arrangement is found on many specimens. Columella and outer lip vary from salmon pink to orange-brown.

SIZE: Length, 3 inches.

RANGE: Florida east coast, Florida west coast-Tampa Bay to Florida Keys.

DESCRIPTION: Shell solid, distinguished by absence of shoulder spines; spire somewhat outstretched; aperture long and narrow; stromboid notch close to base of outer lip; anterior canal short; outer lip winged or much extended; surface sculptured with moderately coarse spiral striae; from the fourth whorl to body-whorl, axial costae produce slightly subsutural spinose sculpturing.

EGG SHELLS

Family OVULIDAE

Members of this family inhabit warm, temperate seas. The animals attach themselves to the branches of the beautifully colored Gorgonias; consequently all forms of these sea plants should be examined for specimens.

The shells are long, narrow, spindle-shaped structures with a correspondingly long, narrow opening.

Genus CYPHOMA Roeding, 1798

Swollen Egg Shell　　Plate VIII, Figure 11　　Cyphoma gibbosa Linné

COLOR: Pure white or white with pale orange longitudinal strip on either side of dorsal center.

SIZE: Length, 1 inch.

RANGE: Florida east coast from Jupiter Inlet southward to Biscayne Bay.

DESCRIPTION: Shell small, thick, elongate-oblong, porcelaneous; spire covered by heavy callus; aperture extends full length of shell but is wider at lower end; outer lip thick; prominent, transverse ridge encircles the shell slightly above the center; surface smooth and highly polished. This family of shells is closely related to the cowries.

Genus SIMNIA (Leach) Risso, 1826

Pointed Egg Shell　　Plate VIII, Figure 12　　Simnia acicularis Lamarck

COLOR: Yellow to deep reddish-purple.

SIZE: Length, 17 mm.

RANGE: Southern Florida east coast to West Indies.

DESCRIPTION: Shell translucent, polished, narrow; ends extended; outer lip thickened at margin, extending full length of shell. This shell and S. uniplicata take on the color of the Georgonia on which it feeds.

Plicate Egg Shell   Plate VIII, Figure 13   Simnia uniplicata Sowerby
COLOR: Yellow to deep reddish-purple.

SIZE: Length, 17 mm.

RANGE: Southern Florida east coast to West Indies.

DESCRIPTION: Shell translucent, tapering, polished; apex slightly recurved over nucleus and produced into short posterior canal; lip thickened; posterior fold conspicuous.

COWRY SHELLS
Family CYPRAEIDAE

Aristocracy of color and form characterize the cowries. Their gracefully curved shells and polished, colorful surfaces have caught the eye of collectors for ages. Modesty and shyness befit these elegantly shelled mollusks, for they usually hide around corals and rocks. No doubt, their conspicuous coloring has proved to be a source of danger. When the mantle of the animal is fully extended, the too large reflected lobes meet over the back of the shell thereby completely concealing it. The calcareous deposit secreted by the mantle produces the elegant surface.

The finished cowry shell is inflated, usually smooth, beautifully painted or patterned, toothed along the elongated aperture, and canaliculated at either end of the opening.

Genus CYPRAEA Linné, 1758

Measled Cowry   Plate IX, Figure 3   Cypraea exanthema Linné

COLOR: Rich yellowish-brown ground with rounded white spots; teeth dark brown; interior pure lavender.

SIZE: Length, 3-4 inches.

RANGE: Southeastern Florida to southern Florida Keys,

DESCRIPTION: Shell moderately thick, smooth, highly polished; body-whorl ventricose; spire very much depressed into body-whorl; aperture extends the full length of the shell and is toothed on both sides; anterior and posterior canals present; surface porcelaneous, richly colored, strikingly patterned. Shells of the genus *Cypraea* are much sought after by shell collectors for they have truly elegant forms.

Yellow spotted Cowry   Plate IX, Figure 4   Cypraea spurca Linné

COLOR: Base white; sides sometimes spotted with brown and yellow; back thickly speckled with yellow.

SIZE: Length, 25-30 mm.

RANGE: Lower east coast of Florida and Florida Keys

DESCRIPTION: Shell thick; aperture extending full length of shell and slightly curved; teeth strong; edges of sides pitted. This is a nicely patterned and colorful cowry.

Genus TRIVIA Gray, 1842

Coffee Bean   Plate VIII, Figure 14   Trivia pediculus Linné

COLOR: Ash-rose pink with brown spots along the dorsal groove.
SIZE: Length, about 10 mm.
RANGE: Central Florida east coast to Florida Keys, southern Florida west coast.

DESCRIPTION: Shell small subglobular; aperture long and narrow; dorsal groove prominent; transverse ribs radiate from dorsal groove around shell into aperture.

Four-Spotted Coffee Bean   Trivia quadripunctata Gray
Plate VIII, Figure 15

COLOR: Flesh-pink becoming deeper pink at the edges and base; four chocolate brown spots along dorsal groove.
SIZE: Length,, about 13 mm.
RANGE: Central Florida east coast to Florida Keys south ern Florida west coast.

DESCRIPTION: Shell similar to T. *pediculus,* but varies some-what in size and color; a brown spot at either end of dorsal groove and one on either side of dorsal groove in middle; ribs fine and regularly arranged.

HELMET SHELLS
Family CASSIDIDAE

Members of the family Cassididae are often referred to as "helmet-shells." They live an active existence, preferably in sandy stations of warm seas where they seek bivalves to satisfy their greedy carni-vorous appetites. An effective radula, dreadful jaws, and good eyes all aid the animal in carrying on its predatory practices on bivalves. The broad, strong foot is well adapted for plowing in sandy sea bottoms.

Helmet shells are solid, usually large, and very ventricose in the region of the body-whorl. The spire is rather flat, but the apex is sharp. A long aperture, extending the full length of the shell ends in a short recurved anterior canal. Teeth are usually located on the inside of the thick outer lip and the columella is either granulated or plicated.

Genus CASSIS Lamarck, 1799
Plate XII, Figures 3, 3a

Queen Helmet Shell	Cassis madagascarensis Lamark
Black Helmet Shell	Cassis madagascarensis Lamarck
Cameo Helmet Shell	Cassis cameo Stimpson

COLOR: Outer surface uniform cream color; interstices between teeth on outer lip, lower portion of outer lip, inside shell wall, inner portion of parietal shield, around and between ridges, and interior of anterior canal are dark chocolate brown; remainder of shield and outer lip deep salmon pink.

SIZE: Length, 4-10 inches.

RANGE: Florida east coast in the region of Lake Worth, and Lower Florida Keys.

DESCRIPTION: Shell large, thick; spire depressed; apex sharp aperture long and narrow; outer lip thick, and equipped with about ten strong white teeth on inner margin; shield broad; upper corner rounded; inner margin has many long, thin, white, ridge-like teeth; anterior canal short and recurved; sculpture consists of numerous spiral ridges and fine, wavy axial growth lines which intersect to give a characteristic surface sculpture; body-whorl has three rows of tubercles of rather uniform size—one row on shoulder and two in the middle portion of the body-whorl. The rich color and large size of this shell make it very striking.

Young specimens of *C. madagascarensis* (about 4 inches long) are often found which show the general characteristics of the adult shell but the body-whorl is indistinctly decorated with light brown bands bearing crescent-shaped marks.

King Helmet Shell   Plate XII, Figures 4, 4a   Cassis tuberosa Linné

COLOR: Buff ground; strips on the outer lip, spaces between the teeth on the outer lip, interior of anterior canal, and spaces between the tooth-like ridges on inside margin of parietal shield area are dark chocolate brown; inside shell wall glazed orange color.

SIZE: Length, 4-10 inches.

RANGE: Florida east coast from Lake Worth to Lower Florida Keys.

DESCRIPTION: Shell large, thick; spire depressed; apex acute; aperture long and narrow; outer lip thick and equipped with about ten strong, white teeth on inner margin; shield broad, upper corner extended out to a rounded point, inner margin has many long, thin, white ridge-like teeth; anterior canal short and recurved; sculpture consists of numerous spiral ridges, and clearly engraved, wavy axial growth lines which cross to give a much finer, netted sculpture than that found on *C. madagascarensis;* body-whorl has three rows of tubercles which are longer and more varied in size than those of *C. madagascarensis.* The first and largest row is on the shoulder, other two rows are developed in the mid region of the body-whorl. This strikingly beautiful shell is often considered the companion shell to *C. madagascarensis.*

Young specimens of *C. tuberosa* (about 4 inches long) are often found which exhibit the same form and sculptural characteristics of the adult shell; but the shield is unfinished and the body-whorl color-pattern is more distinct.

Genus SEMICASSIS Mörch, 1852

Scotch Bonnet   Plate IX, Figure 5   Semicassis granulatum Born

COLOR: Pinkish-white or cream colored ground with squarish brown spots forming a more or less regular pattern; interior medium chestnut color.

SIZE: Length, 60-70 mm.

RANGE: Florida west coast from Sarasota to Marco.

DESCRIPTION: Shell moderately thick, spire moderately high; apex sharp; body-whorl large and rounded; outer lip thick, reflected, and toothed on inner edge; a shield-like callus is attached to the front of the body-whorl—upper portion of shield ridged, lower portion of shield granulated; surface sculptured with deep spirally arranged grooves and flat ridges; anterior canal short and recurved.

Reticulated Helmet Shell   Plate IX, Figure 6   Cassis testiculus Linné

COLOR: Variegated arrangement of flesh color, lavender, red-orange, and brown with squarish patches of brown; lip cream color with a series of pale orange bands curving around the lip and terminating in squarish brown spots; interior of aperture pale orange.

SIZE: Length, 2 to 3 inches.

RANGE: Southern Florida to the West Indies.

DESCRIPTION: Shell thick; body-whorl sculptured with fine longitudinal ridges and grooves which are crossed by more widely separated spiral grooves thereby creating a reticulated surface; outer lip strongly toothed, thickened, and recurved; columella plicated along entire length.

This beautiful species has a wide distribution but is not plentiful.

Flame Helmet Shell   Plate IX, Figure 7   Cassis flammea Linné

COLOR: Creamy white ground marked with dark fawn, moderately large, spirally arranged zigzag patterns; outer, recurved edge of lip marked with brown patches; shield area marked with larger tan patches and zigzag markings.

SIZE: Length, 3 to 5 inches.

RANGE: Southern Florida and Florida Keys.

DESCRIPTION: Shell thick and strong; spire depressed; apex acute; aperture long and narrow; anterior canal short, recurved, and stained with brown on interior; outer lip thickened, moderately recurved; strong white teeth on inner lip margin; interstices colorless; columella equipped with elongated teeth; face shield broad with upper outside corner rounded; surface marked with many axial growth lines which are not cut by conspicuous spiral grooves or ridges; there are usually three graduated rows of tubercles with the largest row on the shoulder. The things which characterize *C. flammea* are colorless interstices on the outer lip, cream colored outer lip, no reticulated sculpture, and a characteristic face shield.

TUN SHELLS
Family TONNIDAE

Mollusks of this family are distributed in warm waters on sandy bottoms. Two strikingly graceful specimens are found in Florida waters.

The animals have a large foot, enlarged mantle and long siphon. The shells are ventricose, have a conspicuously compressed spire, large aperture, and thin flared lip. Spiral grooving is a conspicuous part of the sculpturing.

Genus TONNA Brunnich, 1772

Partridge Tun Shell   Plate IX, Figure 8   Tonna perdix Linné

COLOR: Dark fawn and white speckled pattern disposed into spiral bands on cream-colored ground.

SIZE: Length, 3-5 inches.

RANGE: Southern Florida Keys.

DESCRIPTION: Shell thin, subglobular; body-whorl inflated; spire raised; apex acute; sutures distinctly grooved; outer lip expanded, edge crenulated; umbilicus distinct; sculpture consists of wide spiral grooves and flat rounded ridges crossed by fine axial growth lines.

Genus FICUS Roeding, 1798

Paper Fig Shell   Plate IX, Figure 9   Ficus papyratia Say

COLOR: Dull greyish white; interior glassy, brownish-orange which shows through the translucent shell.

SIZE: Length, 3-4 inches.

RANGE: Florida west coast as far south as Marco Island.

DESCRIPTION: Shell thin, pyriform; spire very depressed; body-whorl much swollen; outer lip thin, flaring; anterior canal elongated; surface sculptured with fine axial ridges and slightly finer spiral ridges which in crossing produce a reticulated surface. This is one of the most gracefully shaped Florida shells.

TRITON SHELLS
Family CYMATIIDAE

Mollusks of this family are taken in warm sea waters. The animal is brilliantly colored. Two characteristic varices, marking rest periods in shell growth, are present on the whorls. The canal is long and the lip is toothed. The family includes among its members the "triton shells" which have featured in religion and literature since the time of ancient Greece. According to Greek legend, the sea demi-god, Triton, did his trumpeting on a triton shell.

Milton alludes to this deity in the song at the conclusion of his *Comus*:

By scaly Triton's winding shell,

and Wordsworth alludes to it in the last stanza of his sonnet *The World Is Too Much With Us*:

Have sight of Proteus rising from the sea;
Or hear old Triton blow his wreathed' horn.

Genus CYMATIUM Roeding, 1798 (Triton of authors)

Angular Triton   Plate IX, Figure 10   Cymatium femorale Linné

DESCRIPTION: Shell elongated, thick; spire high; aperture ovate; anterior canal long and narrow; outer lip greatly flared, thick, edge sculptured with elongated knobs formed at terminations of revolving ridges; columella callused; thickened varix opposite aperture is a prominent feature; surface is coarsely sculptured with heavy noduled revolving ridges and deep wide grooves in which there are fine spiral striae.

MUREX OR ROCK SHELLS
Family MURICIDAE

The Muricidae is a large family of wide distribution. Representatives are found in all seas but the tropical waters hold the most curious and spectacular species. A gravelly, rocky, or coral bottom best suits these voracious sea-robbers. They prey upon all species of mollusks—both univalves and bivalves.

Except for a special gland which secretes a rich bluish-red dye, the animal has a conventional molluscan anatomical structure.

Murex shells are thick and robust. The body-whorl is rather inflated, the spire tapers gradually to an acute apex and the ovate aperture connects with the partially closed canal which ranges in length from short to amazingly long. Conspicuous coloring is not usual in this family; but ornate, elaborate surface sculpture is a striking characteristic of the Muricidae. Varices, nodes, spiney processes, and lacey spiral ridges are prominent sculptural features of the family.

Genus MUREX Linné, 1758

Harvester Murex   Plate X, Figure 1   Murex messorius Sowerby

COLOR: Varies from light to dark tan; occasionally a band of dark tan or brown is developed on the shoulder of last two whorls and base of the body-whorl.

SIZE: Length, 1 to 2 inches.

RANGE: Southern Florida and Florida Keys.

DESCRIPTION: Shell solid; aperture ovate, polished, and white; anterior canal extended, and tapering; outer lip erect along front edge and finely crenulated; columellar callus stands out from the body of the shell in the lower half; sculpture consists of three thickened varices between which are three ridges—two thick and one thin; spiral ridges cross this axial sculpturing and produce a rough knobby surface.

Rose Murex   Plate X, Figure 2   Murex messorius rubidus Baker

DESCRIPTION: Except for the salmon pink color, this shell very closely resembles *M. messorius*. It is most commonly found on the southwest Florida coast.

Apple Murex   Plate IX, Figure 11   Murex pomum Gmelin

COLOR: Exterior surface colored with mottled mixture of white, buff, and brown; spots of dark brown on the fluted edge of varices, outer lip, upper end of columellar lip, and right portion of anterior canal; interior of aperture glazed pink, pale orange, or ivory; col umellar callus colored same as interior of aperture.

SIZE: Length, 2-4 inches.

RANGE: Southern Florida coast and Keys, northward to Tampa Bay in the west and St. Augustine in the east.

DESCRIPTION: Shell thick, rough; body-whorl large; spire comparatively high; aperture ovate; outer lip sharply toothed; an terior canal slightly recurved and flattened on columellar side; col umellar callus attached to body-whorl except for erect edge; axial sculpture consists of three highly elevated, spiny varices with a fluted edge and one or two scaly intervarical ribs; scaly ridges and striae form the spiral sculpture. This species varies greatly as to size and color. Its ornate sculpturing gives it an unusual exterior.

Burnt Rock Shell   Plate IX, Figure 12   Murex florifer Reeve

COLOR: Cream colored ground; spiny varices and revolving ridges are burnt brown or orange color; interior pure white.

SIZE: Length, 2-3 inches.

RANGE: Southern Florida coast and Keys.

DESCRIPTION: Shell thick, spiny; spire moderately high; aper ture circular; outer lip sharp and crenulated; anterior canal broad, semi-enclosed, and flattened on columellar side; right portion of canal spiny; three varices sculptured with long, partially open spines and one knobby intervarical ridge make up the axial sculpture; spiral striae and angular ridges form the spiral sculpture.

Many-Angled Drill   Plate X, Figure 3   Muricidea multangula Philippi

COLOR: Cream colored ground with spirally arranged brown markings; aperture white or pale rose color; epidermis, when present, is dark tan.

SIZE: Length, 20-30 mm.

RANGE: Florida east and west coasts, and Florida Keys.

DESCRIPTION: Shell robust; spire quite elongated; body whorl ventricose; aperture ovate; anterior canal short and compara tively wide; outer lip short and ridged within, surface sculptured with heavy varices which are interrupted at sutures, and do not extend to base of body-whorl; spiral threads cover entire surface.

Genus MURICIDEA Swainson, 1840

Purple Drill   Plate X, Figures 4a, b   Muricidea ostrearum Conrad

COLOR: Light brown or drab purple; purple sutural band; interior of aperture and columella dull, polished purple. Another variety of this shell is pure white.

SIZE: Length, 20-30 mm.

RANGE: Florida west coast—Tampa Bay to Cape Romano.

DESCRIPTION: Shell thin; spire with well shouldered whorls; sutures distinct; whorls well angulated; aperture ovate; outer lip thin; columella thinly callused; axial ribs crossing spiral cords give a nodular surface.

The white variety of this shell is less common than the purple variety. In addition to being pure white, it differs from the purple variety by being slightly larger and thicker; and the sculpturing is slightly stronger.

Genus UROSALPINX Stimpson, 1865

Oyster Drill   Plate X, Figure 5   Urosalpinx cinereus Say

COLOR: White, light yellow, or brown.

SIZE: Length, 1 inch or less.

RANGE: All around the Florida coast where oysters may be found.

DESCRIPTION: Shell small, rough, thin; spire high; aperture ovate; body-whorl sculptured with many fine revolving striae and longitudinal ribs.

Tampa Urosalpinx   Plate X, Figure 6   Urosalpinx tampaensis Conrad

COLOR: White and tan or ash-gray; interior touched with tan.

SIZE: Length, 15-25 mm.

RANGE: Florida West coast—Cedar Keys to Cape Sable.

DESCRIPTION: Shell strong; strong longitudinal ribs overlaid by strong spiral threads produce a coarse, characteristic sculpture; outer lip crenulate; interior of aperture ridged.

PURPLE SHELLS

Family THAISIDAE

This family of mollusks is closely related to the Muricidae in anatomical structure and also has a dye producing property. The shells are coarsely striated or otherwise roughly sculptured.

Open-Mouthed Purple   Plate X, Figure 7   Thais patula Linné

COLOR: Nuclear whorls often cream colored; remaining whorls chocolate brown mottled with cream color around lip region and base of body whorl; columella polished dull orange.

SIZE: Length, 2-3 inches.

RANGE: Florida east coast to West Indies

DESCRIPTION: Shell solid and oblong; spire usually low; body-whorl well-rounded; aperture characteristically capacious; outer lip sharply crenulated, excavated, and flattened; columella is a distinctive part; spirally arranged rows of rough nodules on body-whorl. This is a varied and widely distributed species.

Florida Purple   Plate X, Figure 8   Thais floridana Conrad

COLOR: Dull yellowish-tan ground with bands of fine revolving pencil lines of brown; columella, outer lip, and interior are yellow-orange or pale pink.

SIZE: Length, 1-2 inches.

RANGE: Florida Gulf, southern, and east coasts.

DESCRIPTION: Shell oblong, solid; whorls few; spire comparatively high; apex sharp; anterior canal slightly recurved; suture grooved; columella, lip and interior, are smooth and polished; sculpturing consists of fine ridges and striae and low tubercles on shoulder of whorls.

Family PYRENIDAE (Columbellidae)

This is a family of mollusks which is adapted to warm, mostly tropical waters. They may be taken in any depth from five fathoms to the littoral region.

The shells are small, the spire moderately high, and the apex acute. The aperture is narrow. The outer lip is thickened and dentate within. The coloring and sculpture vary greatly in the different species but is not striking.

Genus PYRENE Roeding, 1798
Subgenus COLUMBELLA Lamarck, 1799

Trader Pyrene   Plate X, Figure 9   Pyrene mercatoria Linné

COLOR: Color variable; sometimes exterior surface is colored with mottled and speckled arrangement of black and white; exterior of outer lip usually white; interior pure white.

SIZE: Length, 15 mm.

RANGE: Florida east coast.

DESCRIPTION: Shell small, solid; spire elevated; apex sharp; body-whorl elongated; aperture is a long, narrow slit; outer lip curved inward, thickened especially in the middle, and conspicuously toothed; columella toothed on lower portion, two or three teeth at upper end; surface sculptured with fine, flat, slightly beaded spiral ridges.

Genus **MITRELLA** Risso, 1826

Lunar-Marked Columbella   Mitrella lunata Say

Plate X, Figure 10

COLOR: Brown and white with crescent-shaped whitish spots.
SIZE: Length, 5-10 mm.
RANGE: Florida east and southern coasts.
DESCRIPTION: Shell small, smooth; aperture oblong; outer lip toothed within. It is often found at low-tide mark and on shallow sandy bottoms.

BASKET SHELLS
Family **NASSARIIDAE**

The animals of the Nassariidae are carnivorous and often prey upon the egg capsules of other mollusks.

The small, oval-shaped shells have prominent sculpturing. The spire is sharp, the columellar callus is thick and polished, and the anterior canal is short.

Genus **NASSARIUS** Dumeril, 1805

Blown Basket Shell   Plate X, Figure 11   Nassarius vibex Say

COLOR: Spirally arranged tan and brown bands on a dull background; callus and outer edge of lip white.
SIZE: Length, 10 mm.
RANGE: Florida west coast to West Indies.
DESCRIPTION: Shell small, thick, ovate; apex acute; body-whorl much swollen; aperture subcircular; anterior canal short, recurved; axial ribs and spiral striae produce a strong rough sculpture. This species is abundant in sandy, quiet pools and bays.

WHELK SHELLS
Family **BUCCINIDAE**

Animals of this family are carnivorous. The shells are ovate and characteristically sculptured. The posterior canal is conspicuous.

Genus **CANTHARUS** Roeding, 1798

Painted Cantharus   Plate X, Figure 12   Cantharus tinctus Conrad

COLOR: Variegated pattern of yellow-orange, lavender, and grayish-brown.

SIZE: Height, 25 mm.

RANGE: Littoral regions of all Florida shores.

DESCRIPTION: Shell ovate, thick, sculptured with a system of revolving ridges and prominent axial ribs; aperture oval; outer lip thick and finely crenulated on inner edge; anterior canal short; posterior canal formed by top tooth on lip and porcelaneous ridge at top of columella.

NEPTUNE SHELLS

Family **NEPTUNEIDAE**

Members of the family Neptuneidae are distributed in a variety of geographic provinces. Consequently their forms vary greatly in shape and surface decoration, as a result of adaptation to environmental differences. It is not a colorful family, but Floridian representatives of the genera *Busycon* and *Melongena* have pretty though not striking color patterns.

Genus **BUSYCON** Roeding, 1798 (Fulgur of authors)

Channeled Whelk   Plate IX, Figure 13   Busycon canaliculatus Say

COLOR: Exterior streaked with dull orange and white; interior of aperture is a polished yellow-orange; epidermis brown.

SIZE: Length, 5-6 inches.

RANGE: Florida east coast.

DESCRIPTION: Shell large, pyriform; whorls have flat shoulders and nearly vertical sides; sutures deeply channeled; periphery of whorls flatly noduled; body-whorl marked with rough irregular growth lines; anterior canal elongated; outer lip sharp. This is one of the most gracefully shaped Florida shells.

Left-Handed Whelk   Plate IX, Figure 14   Busycon perversum Linné

COLOR: Young specimens have cream-colored ground and lightning-like axial streaks of chestnut color; interior is polished, pinkish-white. Old specimens lack color pattern; exterior is usually a drab, chalky white; interior polished cream color.

SIZE: Length, 2-12 inches.

RANGE: Florida west coast and southwest coast.

DESCRIPTION: Shell heavy, pear-shaped, sinistral; spire short; apex sharp; sutures distinct; body-whorl large above and tapering into a long narrow anterior canal; outer lip sharp-edged, lined within; spiral sculpturing consists of strong cords and striae—especially in the region of the shoulder and canal; shoulders usually tuberculated This shell is easily identified because of the aperture being on the left side.

Pear Whelk   Plate IX, Figure 15   Busycon pyrum Dillwyn

COLOR: White ground streaked with longitudinal stripes of brown.

SIZE: Length, 2-4 inches.

RANGE: Florida Gulf Coast, especially on sandy bottom of littoral region.

DESCRIPTION: Shell thin, smooth, pyriform; spire flattened; sutures deeply grooved; aperture large; lip simple and thin-edged; anterior canal long; fine spiral lines form the surface sculpture.

Genus **MELONGENA** Schumacher, 1817

King's Crown Conch   Plate IX, Figure 16   Melongena corona Gmelin

COLOR: Wavy, spiral bands of brown and white on white ground; interior of aperture and columellar callus, milky white.

SIZE: Length, 3 inches.

RANGE: Florida west and east coasts.

DESCRIPTION: Shell solid; spire short; body-whorl large and gracefully curved; aperture ovate; anterior canal short and wide; outer lip thin; columella callused; shoulders slightly concave; sharp, curved, excavated spines decorate periphery of body-whorl and one or two succeeding whorls; base of body-whorl often equipped with same type of spines. The size, sculpture, and color of this shell is extremely variable. A marine algae growth often clouds the color and sculpture.

BAND SHELLS
Family **FASCIOLARIIDAE**

The family Fasciolariidae has among its members some species which are very distinctive either for their great size or beauty of form. *Fasciolaria gigantea* is believed to be the largest known univalve shell, and *Fasciolaria tulipa* and *distans* are conspicuous for their beauty of color and pattern.

The animals are in no way extraordinary; they are slow of motion and shy of nature. They prey upon both bivalves and univalves.

Their shells are solid and fusiform with a gracefully tapered spire and a very long anterior canal. The outer lip is simple and the columella is plicate.

Genus FASCIOLARIA Lamarck, 1801

Giant Band Shell   Plate XII, Figure 5   Fasciolaria gigantea Kiener

COLOR: Pale fawn color or dull pinkish-white; interior bright orange or dusky ivory; epidermis, dark brown.

SIZE: Length, 8-16 inches.

RANGE: Southern Florida, northward along the west coast to Cedar Keys and along the east coast to Indian River.

DESCRIPTION: Shell large, thick, fusiform; spire high; aperture large and tapering into long, open, anterior canal; surface roughened by coarse spiral ridges and nodose axial ribs—largest nodes in region of shoulder. This is the largest known gasteropod shell.

Young Giant Band Shells   Fasciolaria gigantia Kiener
Plate XI, Figure 1

Young specimens of *F. gigantia* (from 1-2 inches long) are often found on the beaches which are similar in form and general sculpturing to the adult shell. They do not, however, exhibit the finished sculpturing of the adult shell; and the most common colors are pale yellow, pure orange, and burnt orange.

Tulip Band Shell   Plate XI, Figures 2a, b   Fasciolaria tulipa Linné

COLOR: Variable; usually a variegated pattern of white and olive brown; fine interrupted spiral lines of brown. Orange colored specimens are less common.

SIZE: Length, 4-6 inches.

RANGE: Florida Gulf coast.

DESCRIPTION: Shell spindle-shaped; spire tapered; collumella curved, and equipped with two to three plications on lower portion; spiral sculpture consists of flat ridges becoming angled and coarse near sutures; axial growth lines also mark surface. This is one of the most gracefully shaped and prettily patterned Floridian shells.

Pale Tulip   Plate XI, Figure 3   Fasciolaria distans **Lamarck**

COLOR: Marbleized color pattern of white, grey, and light brown on which distinct dark brown spiral lines are laid.

SIZE: Length, 2-3 inches.

RANGE: Florida Gulf coast.

DESCRIPTION: This species differs from *F. tulipa* in its smaller size, smoother surface, and uninterrupted color lines of dark brown. The general shape of the two species is similar.

VASE SHELLS
Family XANCIDAE

Members of this family are adapted to warm sea waters. The shells of Xancidae are thick, the spire is much flattened, the apex is acute, and the columella is plicate.

Genus VASUM Roeding, 1798

Rough Vase Shell   Plate XI, Figure 4   Vasum muricatum **Born**

COLOR: White or white with brown, irregular, longitudinal lines on body-whorl and shoulder of body whorl; interior porcelaneous white or white mixed with brown; epidermis brown.

SIZE: Length, 2-3 inches.

RANGE: Florida Keys.

DESCRIPTION: Shell solid, thick, triangular-shaped; spire abruptly tapered; apex acute; body-whorl tapers down to a narrow base with slightly recurved canal; aperture elongated; columella plicated in central portion; sculpture consists of one to three rows of sharp tubercles around periphery of whorls and one to three rows of tubercles about the base; coarse spiral ridges and striae around body-whorl.

VOLUTE SHELLS
Family VOLUTIDAE

Rarity, extraordinary beauty of form, and unusual patterning make the shells of this family very aristocratic and much sought after. Very little is known of the animal's habits, but they are believed to be rock dwellers: consequently they are not reached with dredges.

Genus **MACULOPEPLUM** Dall, 1906

Juno's Volute   Plate XI, Figure 5   Maculopeplum junonia **Hwass**

COLOR: Ivory white ground decorated with spiral rows of squarish brown spots; interior, delicate salmon pink.

SIZE: Length, 2-4 inches.

RANGE: Florida Gulf coast from Tampa Bay to the southern Florida Keys; deep water off Palm Beach.

DESCRIPTION: Shell elongate, smooth, gracefully tapered at both ends; suture well defined; outer lip thin-edged but thickened within; columella ridged with four plaits and involute. A shell of this species is a rare addition to any collection.

MARGIN SHELLS
Family MARGINELLIDAE

This is a family of dainty little sand dwelling, warm sea mollusks which can often be taken between tide-marks.

The animals are marked with gay colored spots which make them appear as attractive as their shells. The siphon is long, the foot large, and the mantle, when the animal is extended, covers a portion of the shell.

The shells are polished. The body-whorl is comparatively large, the spire short, the aperture narrow, and the outer lip thickened. If these shells were not so small and abundant, their beauty would be much more appreciateed.

Genus **MARGINELLA** Lamarck, 1801

Pointed Marginella   Plate X, Figure 13   Marginella apicina **Menke**

COLOR: Usually yellow with indistinct blended bands of light fawn color; outer lip white with dark brown spots on outer edge.

SIZE: Length, about 14 mm.

RANGE: Florida Gulf coast.

DESCRIPTION: Shell small highly polished, smooth; spire depressed; apex sharp; body-whorl comparatively large; aperture long, narrow; outer lip much thickened; lower part of columella has four plaits. This marginella is abundant in shallow sandy regions.

Plate X, Figure 14   Marginella veliei **Pilsbry**

COLOR: Pale yellow; outer lip, collumellar folds, and sutural line, white.

SIZE: Length, 12-15 mm.

RANGE: Florida west coast.

DESCRIPTION: Shell small, slender, thin, polished, translucent; apex acute; sutures clear and marked by fine thread-like lines, aperture elongated; outer lip thickened; columella marked with four folds on lower portion. It is found most frequently in shallow water on sandy bottoms.

OLIVE SHELLS
Family OLIVIDAE

The family Olividae is of subtropical and tropical distribution. The shells are subcylindrical and highly polished; the spire is short, the body-whorl extremely elongated, the aperture is long and narrow, and the lip is simple.

Genus OLIVA Bruguiere, 1789

Lettered Olive   Plate X, Figures 15a, b   Oliva sayana Ravenel

COLOR: Creamy-white ground on which an angled and zig-zag pattern of fine light brown lines is laid.

SIZE: Length, 1-2 inches.

RANGE: Florida west coast.

DESCRIPTION: Shell thick and subcylindrical; spire short; sutures channeled; body-whorl elongated; aperture long and deeply notched at base; lip simple and smooth-edged; columella is thickly callused and equipped with oblique folds on lower portion, one plication revolves obliquely about lower portion of shell; surface smooth, highly polished and porcelaneous. Everyone admires the polished beauty of this shell.

Golden-Yellow Olive Shell   Oliva sayana citrina Johnson

COLOR: Golden-yellow.

SIZE: Length, 50 mm.

RANGE: Florida Gulf coast.

DESCRIPTION: This is the form of *O. sayana* which is pure yellow-orange. It is rather rare and very beautiful. Sandy, shallow regions are the best places to look for it.

Genus OLIVELLA

Rice Shell   Plate X, Figures 16a, b   Olivella floralia Duclos

COLOR: Polished white, apex sometimes tinged with yellow.

SIZE: Length, 12-20 mm.

RANGE: Southern Florida east coast; Florida Keys; to West Indies.

DESCRIPTION: Shell slender, translucent, highly polished; spire much tapered; apex acute; body-whorl elongated; aperture about half as long as entire shell; outer lip simple; columella callused and finely plicated.

AUGER SHELLS
Family TEREBRIDAE

The shells of this family have a long, tapering spire with many whorls. The short subovate aperture ends in a recurved notch. Members of this group are found in subtropical and tropical waters, usually in shallow, sandy regions.

Genus TEREBRA Bruguiere, 1798

Dislocated Auger Shell   Plate X, Figure 17   Terebra disclocata Say
COLOR: Grey or light brown.
SIZE: Length, 1-2 inches.
RANGE: Florida Gulf and east coasts on sandy bottom.
DESCRIPTION: Shell turret-shaped; apex sharp; aperture small; outer lip thin-edged; basal notch recurved; surface sculptured with numerous axial ridges interrupted by spiral grooves and bands.

Wine-Colored Auger Shell   Terebra concava vinosa Dall
Plate X, Figure 18

COLOR: Mixture of tan, grey, and vinous tints.
SIZE: Length, 20 mm.
RANGE: Florida Gulf, southern, and east coasts.
DESCRIPTION: Shell slender, much tapered; aperture small; outer lip simple; canal short and recurved; surface beautifully sculptured with longitudinal ribs and a bead-like spiral band at suture. General characteristics are similar to those of *T. Disclocata.*

Auger Shell   Plate X, Figure 19   Terebra protexta Conrad
COLOR: Pale brown or orange on lower part of whorls, lighter tone on sutural band.
SIZE: Length, 1-1.5 inches.
RANGE: Florida Gulf, south, and east coasts.
DESCRIPTION: General characteristics of the shell are those of the genus *Terebra;* whorls are slightly more convex, and sutural band has less conspicuous sculpturing.

CONE SHELLS
Family CONIDAE

This is a family of mollusks which prefer to live around the rocky, reefy bottoms of tropical seas.

The shells of Conidae are—as the name indicates—cone shaped. The handsomest species have vivid colors and interesting patterns. The body-whorl is long and tapering. The apex is sharp. The aperture which extends the full length of the body-whorl has a posterior notch for the accommodation of the canal.

Genus CONUS Linné, 1758

Florida Chinese Alphabet Cone   Conus spurius atlanticus (new
Plate XI, Figure 6   subspecies)
Conus proteus Hwass (of authors)

COLOR: White ground; orange or dark brown dots, squares and dashes are arranged or merged into more or less regular spiral bands; interior porcelaneous white; epidermis thin brown.

SIZE: Length, 2-3 inches.

DESCRIPTION: Shell smooth, solid; spire much depressed; apex pointed; sutures well defined; outer lip sharp and straight; aperture long and narrow; shell shoulder very flat; sculpture consists of fine growth lines which are somewhat coarser than the fine spiral lines. Sand bars and grassy flats of inside waters are places where this species is often found.

Florida Cone   Plate XI, Figure 7   Conus floridanus Gabb

COLOR: White ground; two clear orange or dusky yellow spiral bands on body-whorl, banded color disposed into irregular patches: a white thin band with orange dots usually separates the two colored bands; streaks of orange or dusky yellow decorate the spire.

SIZE: Length, 1.5-2 inches.

RANGE: Florida west coast, especially southwest Florida.

DESCRIPTION: Shell smooth and strong; spire much more elevated than in the Florida Chinese Alphabet Shell, and somewhat concave; outer lip thin-edged and indented above; sculpture consists of minute growth lines on body-whorl and spire, and fine engraved grooves about base of shell. Although this species is common on the Florida west coast, it is rare elsewhere.

Stearns' Cone   Plate XI, Figure 8   Conus stearnsi Conrad

COLOR: Dull white marked with drab, brownish mottling. Spirally arranged rows of fine broken lines of reddish-brown and white are characteristic markings.

SIZE: Length, 18-20 mm.

RANGE: Florida Gulf coast and Florida east coast.

DESCRIPTION: Shell characteristically cone-shaped; spire high with distinct, sharply angled whorls; apex acute; body-whorl sharply shouldered and sculptured with finely incised, regularly arranged, spiral lines on the lower half which are sometimes continued into the upper portion but are faintly incised; aperture long and narrow; outer lip finely crenulated in lower region where incised lines terminate.

Striped Florida Cone   Conus floridanus floridensis Sowerby
                      Plate XI, Figure 9

COLOR: White with patches of reddish-brown. Numerous superimposed spiral rows of reddish-brown dots and dashes or continuous lines constitute a characteristic pattern.

SIZE: Length, 30-35 mm.

RANGE: Florida Gulf coast and Florida east coast.

DESCRIPTION: This shell is very similar and often confused with *C. Floridanus;* but it is distinguished from it by having a darker reddish-brown background color instead of yellow-orange and by having numerous, superimposed spiral lines.

CROSS-BARRED SHELLS
Family CANCELLARIIDAE

This small family is characterized by having shells with a conspicuously cancellated surface and strongly plicated columella.

Genus CANCELLARIA Lamarck, 1799

Cross-Barred or Nutmeg Shell   Cancellaria conradiana Dall
                      Plate XI, Figure 10

COLOR: Mixture of white and variegated shades of brown arranged to give the effect of spiral bands and longitudinal stripes.

SIZE: 25-35 mm.

RANGE: Florida west coast.

DESCRIPTION: Shell oval, robust; spire high; apex sharp; body-whorl ventricose; interior ribbed; anterior canal wide and short;

outer lip thin and finely crenulated; columella equipped with three prominent plaits. The series of spiral ridges and axial ridges creates a regular beaded or reticulated surface.

BUBBLE SHELLS
Family BULLIDAE

Members of the family Bullidae have become adapted to a wide range in warm sea depths. The shells are of medium size and are cylindrical, the spire is rolled inward, the apex is perforate, and the aperture extends beyond the length of the body-whorl.

Genus BULLA Linné, 1758
Florida Bubble   Plate X, Figure 20   Bulla occidentalis C. B. Adams

COLOR: Mottled or speckled pattern of variegated browns on a white ground.

SIZE: Length, 20-25 mm.

RANGE: Widely distributed around Florida coast.

DESCRIPTION: Shell smooth; spire involute; outer lip produced beyond length of body-whorl. This species is abundant in Florida waters, especially in sandy stations.

Family ELLOBIIDAE

Members of this family live a double or amphibious life. They can live for many hours out of water because they can breath air, but they need some form of moisture. Salt marshes and brackish water regions are favorable localities for them. The shells are ovate, aperture long, columella strongly plicated, and outer lip usually toothed within.

Genus MELAMPUS Montfort, 1810
Coffee Shell   Plate X, Figure 21   Melampus coffeus Linné

COLOR: Dull olive-green or grey; narrow white shoulder band. sometimes one or two white bands about middle of body-whorl; epidermis thin brown.

SIZE: Length, 18 mm.

RANGE: Florida west coast from Tampa Bay area down to southern Florida.

DESCRIPTION: Shell oval, strong smooth; spire flattened; apex sharp; body-whorl comparatively ventricose; aperture extends the length of the body-whorl but is wider at base; outer lip sharp and ridged within; columella has two folds—upper one porcelaneous white and much thickened. This species is commonly found in mud flats and salt marshes.

Class CEPHALOPODA

High organization and intelligence put the *Cephalopoda* in a rather segregated place in the phylum Mollusca. However, the arrangement of organs and the presence of a mantle and radula account for the molluscan classification. Nautilus, Octopus, Spirula, cuttlefish and squid are among its members. Not all of these, hower, are represented in Floridian waters, but an observing and persistent collector can expect to encounter the Paper Nautilus, *Argonauta argo,* and *Spirula spirula.*

Size variations among the species of the class are incredible. They range all the way from little one inch sepiolas and one foot squids to the giant, dangerous, fifty foot octopus so imaginatively and compellingly described by Victor Hugo in *The Toilers of the Sea.*

Superior anatomical structure is observed in all members of the class. The word *Cephalopoda*—meaning "feet about the head" —describes one distinctive anatomical feature. A constricted strip, suggestive of a neck, separates the head on which the two distinct eyes are placed. On the head above the eyes is the foot. The foot is divided into eight or ten arm-like, sucker-bearing appendages on the upper side, and a funnel-like tube on the under side. The latter part acts as an organ of expulsion through which water is expelled from the mantle cavity. A cup-shaped, muscular mantle covers the animals's body leaving only the anterior end open for the extension of the head and funnel. Pigment-cells for protective purposes cover the mantle surface. By rapid, willful adjustment of these cells (chromatophores) the animal is able to adjust its color to its surroundings. A curious ink-sac possessed by certain cephalopods also has a protective purpose. The animal by ejecting this brown fluid from its funnel can escape from danger in a cloud of color. This secretion from the genus Sepia has an extensive commercial value.

The only form of the cephalopod group having the external shell so characteristic of mollusks is Nautilus. All other forms have some kind of internal shell. Spirula's small internal shell is chambered.

Family SPIRULIDAE
Genus SPIRULA Lamarck, 1799

Spiral Shell

Spirula spirula Linné

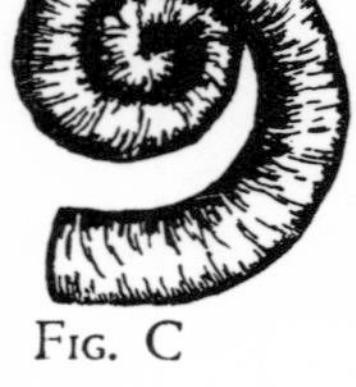

FIG. C

COLOR: Nacreous white.
SIZE: Width, about 1 inch.
RANGE: Open waters of Florida Key region.
DESCRIPTION: Shell internal, small, and chambered; the two or three whorls scarcely touch.

DESCRIPTIONS OF SHELLS ILLUSTRATED
IN PLATES XIII AND XIV

ARK SHELLS

Family ARCIDAE

Genus ARCA Linné, 1758

Beaked Ark   Plate XIII, Figures 1a, b   Arca umbonata Lamarck

COLOR: Exterior tannish-white near umbones shading into brownish-purple, concentric markings; interior opaque white tinged with dull purple; epidermis tan.

SIZE: Length, 1-2 inches.

RANGE: North Carolina to the Gulf of Mexico.

DESCRIPTION: Shell elongate, inflated, medium thick; equivalve, and inequilateral; umbones placed wide apart, conspicuous, recurved; anterior end of shell rounded, posterior end strongly ridged; hinge margin straight; ventral margin curved; byssal notch below umbones; ribs on posterior keel six to eight and distinct; remaining surface irregularly cross-ribbed to give a beaded effect to radial lines; space between umbones diamond-shaped; interior surface smooth. This species lives in moderately deep waters—three to seven fathoms.

Genus GLYCYMERIS DaCosta, 1778

Comb Bittersweet   Glycymeris pectinata Gmelin

Plate XIII, Figures 2a, b

COLOR: Exterior white with irregular purplish-brown rib markings that give the effect of interrupted concentric bands; interior white stained with purplish-brown from the muscle scar area to the ventral pallial line.

SIZE: Length and height, 15-21 mm.

RANGE: North Carolina to the West Indies and west to Mexico.

DESCRIPTION: Shell solid, orbicular, slightly inflated; equivalve and equilateral; umbones are central, small, pointed, and slightly parted; hinge region narrow; about ten comb-like hinge teeth on either side of the beak margin; margins crenulated; the twenty to twenty-four radial ribs are crossed by thread-like growth lines, posterior and anterior ribs are finer than mid-ribs. This species favors sandy bottom at a depth of two to six fathoms.

MUSSEL SHELLS

Family MYTILIDAE
Genus MODIOLUS Lamarck, 1799

Paper Mussel   Plate XIII, Figure 3   Modiolus aborescens Dillwyn

COLOR: Exterior pale, iridescent green marked with faint zigzag lines of purple; interior nacreous.

SIZE: Length, 22-32 mm.

RANGE: Florida east and west coasts, especially in the mud of inside waters.

DESCRIPTION: Shell irregularly oblong, fragile; equivalve—longest from umbones diagonally across to opposite margin; decidedly inequilateral; umbones small, far anterior, but not terminal; hinge margin straight; surface smooth and polished; epidermis thin and scaly.

Genus BOTULA Mörch, 1853

Chestnut Mussel   Plate XIII, Figure 4   Botula castanea Say

COLOR: Exterior, blue-violet mostly concealed by a glossy, brown, lacquer-like epidermis; interior lavender shading into deeper purple in umbonal region.

SIZE: Length, 15 mm.

RANGE: North Carolina south to Florida, West Indies, and Florida Gulf coast, especially in shallow to moderate depth waters.

DESCRIPTION: Shell broadly elliptical, inflated in umbonal region, fragile, smooth; umbones elevated, far forward, nearly touching; anterior and posterior margins rounded; byssal notch depressed.

Genus LITHOPHAGA Roeding, 1798

Date Shells: The close resemblance of these shells to seeds of dates explains the common name. Large species reach a size of two inches. The shell is thin, cylindrical, elongate, and wedge-shaped if viewed from above. The ligament is internal and there are no teeth. The umbones are situated near the rounded anterior end and are very inconspicuous. Young date shells attach themselves to objects by a byssus, but adult shells bore into limestone and soft rocks.

Scissor Date   Plate XIII, Figure 5   Lithophaga aristata Dillwyn

COLOR: Dull greyish-white with smooth, thin, brown epidermis.

SIZE: Length, 20 mm.

RANGE: North Carolina to the Gulf of Mexico.

DESCRIPTION: Shell shows general characteristics of the genus, but it is smaller than some species. A distinguishing feature is the scissor-like way in which the posterior extensions on the valves are crossed. These mollusks like to bore into coral and soft rock.

GRECIAN EVE SHELLS
Family PANDORIDAE

These curious little shells are very inequivalve. The right valve is flat and the left valve is convex. The internal ligament is fastened in an oblique groove. The umbones are tiny. These clams are widely distributed throughout the seas.

Genus PANDORA Hwass, 1795

Sand Pandora   Plate XIII, Figures 6a, b   Pandora arenosa Conrad

COLOR: Exterior white; interior pearly.

SIZE: Length, 12 mm.

RANGE: From Nova Scotia on the east Atlantic coast to the Gulf of Mexico.

DESCRIPTION: Right valve slightly concave, left valve convex; anterior and ventral margins curved; posterior portion of shell extended and curved slightly upward; surface of right valve marked with finely etched radial lines; left valve sculptured with characteristic growth lines. This pellucid, pearly little clam is delicate enough to be blown about.

ROCK OYSTER SHELLS
Family CHAMIDAE
Genus CHAMA Linné, 1758

Congregate Chama   Plate XIII, Figures 7a, b   Chama congregata Conrad

COLOR: Rose and yellow specimens are found. The deepest tones are on the lacy foliations. Interior is china-white except where exterior color extends in toward the pallial border.

SIZE: Length, 22 mm.

RANGE: Tampa, Florida, to West Indies.

DESCRIPTION: Shell rounded, solid, strikingly inequilateral; attached or left valve is larger and deeper; external ligament follows curve of the umbones; one strong cardinal tooth in upper valve; margins delicately and sharply crenulate. The crossing of radial ribs and foliate growth lines gives the effect of lacy layers.

These shells present many irregularities because they grow fast to some of the most disorderly masonry of the ocean's floor; yet when their environment is favorable, they develop exquisite ornamentation.

LUCINA SHELLS

Family **LUCINIDAE**
Genus **LUCINA** Bruguière, 1797
Asbestos Lucina   Plate XIII, Figures 8a, b   Lucina amiantus Dall

COLOR: White inside and out.

SIZE: Length, 5 mm.

RANGE: Florida west coast and scattered east coast locations.

DESCRIPTION: Shell tiny, nearly round, solid, slightly inflated; umbones distinct and pointed but small; lunule is tiny and clearly outlined; cardinal and lateral teeth present; sculpture consists of about twelve distinct radial ribs crossed by fine, regular, concentric lines. This species favors sandy or muddy bottom ranging from shallow to deep water. Although inconspicuous by size, its definite sculpturing and precise shape make it easy to distinguish from other species.

COCKLE SHELLS

Family **CARDIIDAE**
Genus **LAEVICARDIUM** Swainson, 1840
Morton's Cockle   Plate XIII, Figures 9a, b   Laevicardium mortoni Conrad

COLOR: The exterior of adult shells is creamy white. Young specimens are often marked with zigzag patches of dark fawn-color. The interior coloration shows much variation. The margins are usually white. The main cavity color of clear yellow is often flecked with orange or purple. A purple patch on the posterior side is a distinguishing coloration.

SIZE: Length, 17 mm.

RANGE: From Massachusetts to Brazil in the east and from Cedar Keys to the West Indies in the west.

DESCRIPTION: Shell small, obliquely-ovate in shape, thin but not fragile, inflated; equivalve; smooth and polished inside and out; umbones rounded and high; ligament long and comparatively strong; margins finely serrate; exterior surface marked with faint concentric lines crossed by equally faint radial ribs. This strikingly pretty little shell is often found in the mud and sand close to shore.

VENUS SHELLS

Family **VENERIDAE**
Genus **CYCLINELLA** Dall, 1902
Circular Venus   Plate XIII, Figures 10a, b   Cyclinella tenuis Récluz

COLOR: Its alabastrine white gives it distinction even without color. The epidermis, when present, is thin and pale fawn-color.

SIZE: Length, 1 inch.

RANGE: Cedar Keys, Florida, south to the West Indies.

DESCRIPTION: Shell circular, translucent, thin but not fragile, inflated in umbonal region; equivalve, slightly inequilateral; umbones small and curved forward; three cardinal teeth in each valve; margins are smooth, rounded, and sharp as a knife; pallial sinus directed toward umbones. This elegant little venus shell prefers sandy bottom at about two fathoms.

Genus CHIONE Megerle von Mühlfeld, 1811
Patterned Venus   Plate XIII, Figure 11   Chione intapurpurea Conrad

COLOR: Exterior ivory color mottled with more or less regular patterns of variegated brown; lunule and escutcheon brown; interior mid-area and umbonal cavity red-violet—deepest near posterior side; ventral margin often white.

SIZE: Length, 1⅜ inches.

RANGE: Cape Hatteras to Florida and along the Gulf coast.

DESCRIPTION: Shell oblong-oval in outline, robust and moderately thick; escutcheon flat; lunule well defined; umbones curved forward, conspicuous and low; ventral margin characteristically convex; interior smooth with crenate margin. The sculpturing of this species is remarkably elegant. Many rounded, concentric ridges in the mid-area of the valves become strongly lamellated in the posterior and anterior areas. Many of these have a graceful way of fading out before reaching the lunule and escutcheon margins. Fine radial lines complete the sculpturing. They are distinct in the interstices but do not cross the concentric ridges. This species has the same general shape and characteristics as C. cancellata but it lacks the high, sharp cross-bars. Its sculpturing is generally finer.

Genus VENUS Linné, 1758
Marked Venus   Plate XIII, Figures 12a, b   Venus mercenaria notata Say

COLOR: The color of this clam differs from its close relative— V. mercenaria—only in having brown zigzag lines and patches on the exterior and in not having the interior violet tinges.

SIZE: Length, 3 to 4 inches.

RANGE: Extensive range: Massachusetts to Florida and along the coast of the Gulf of Mexico.

DESCRIPTION: This subspecies of V. mercenaria shows all the usual characteristics of the family. It is, however, a smaller variety. Its distinguishing feature is the zigzag pattern which on fresh specimens is very clear.

TELLIN SHELLS
Family **TELLINIDAE**
Genus **TELLINA** Linné, 1758

Wood's Tellin   Plate XIII, Figure 13   Tellina interrupta Wood

COLOR: Cream color with ray-like streaks of brown patterned with zigzag lines of brown; interior clear, polished yellow except for white border.

SIZE: Length, 2-3 inches.

RANGE: North Carolina to Brazil.

DESCRIPTION: Shell elongate, flattened, unpolished; anterior end well rounded; posterior end rostrate and curved to the right; umbones suppressed and nearly central; two cardinal teeth and lateral plates in each valve; pallial sinus deep and well curved; surface sculptured with raised concentric ridges which are slightly lamellated over the posterior and anterior areas. This species is easily distinguished from other tellin shells.

Linen Tellin   Plate XIII, Figure 14   Tellina lintea Conrad

COLOR: Pure white.

SIZE: Length, 19 mm. to 1 inch

RANGE: North Carolina to the Gulf of Mexico.

DESCRIPTION: Shell small, thin, flattened; anterior and ventral region gracefully rounded; posterior end rostrate, truncate and straight margined; umbones tiny and sharp; surface finely sculptured with concentric lines which become raised around the anterior and ventral margins to give the effect of a border. This delicate little shell is nearly as broad as it is tall.

BEACH or SURF CLAM SHELLS
Family **MACTRIDAE**
Genus **ANATINA** Schumacher, 1817

Lined Duck   Plate XIII, Figure 15   Anatina lineata Say

COLOR: Exterior dull white; interior polished white; epidermis glossy, dull yellow.

SIZE: Length, 2-3 inches.

RANGE: New Jersey to the Gulf of Mexico and south to South America.

DESCRIPTION: Shell thin, fragile, inflated; inequilateral; anterior area widely rounded; posterior area sculptured with a sharp radiating ridge; posterior margin flared and gaping; umbones directed forward and high; surface decorated with irregular, raised, string-like growth lines. This shell is about the same size as A. canaliculata but not as common.

ANGEL WING SHELLS

Family **PHOLADIDAE**
Genus **MARTESIA** Leach, 1825
Wood Piddock   Plate XIII, Figures 16a, b   Martesia striata Linné

COLOR: Greyish-white.

SIZE: Length, 18-35 mm.

RANGE: South Carolina to the West Indies.

DESCRIPTION: Shell wedge-shaped, thin, brittle; posterior end prolonged to a rounded tip; anterior margin slightly parted; a shallow groove separates the posterior from the anterior region; anterior-dorsal margin is recurved over the umbonal region; posterior plate (protoplax) is usually trilobed; anterior region is sculptured with regular elevated, wavy lines which are crossed in the umbonal area by minute radial lines; posterior region shows flatter and less regular growth lines. These wood-boring bivalves will penetrate water-soaked wood to a depth of one inch by means of the foot. Old timbers along beaches should be checked for them.

TOOTH SHELLS

Family **DENTALIIDAE**
Genus **DENTALIUM** Linné, 1758
Ivory Tooth Shell   Plate XIV, Figure 1   Dentalium eboreum Conrad

COLOR: Highly polished white with some dense white areas; fresh specimens are salmon pink.

SIZE: Length, 25-38 mm; diameter, 2-3 mm.

RANGE: North Carolina to the Gulf of Mexico and West Indies.

DESCRIPTION: Shell thin but not fragile or brittle, gradually curved, gradually tapered to sharp posterior tip; circular in cross-section; apical end marked by about twenty minute lines. The characteristic apical slit on the convex side is often broken or worn off.

TOP SHELLS

Family **TROCHIDAE**
Genus **CALLIOSTOMA** Swainson, 1840
Tiny Top Shell   Plate XIV, Figures 2a, b   Calliostoma veliei Pilsbry

COLOR: Light tan ground, patterned with regularly arranged, red-violet streaks; pure tan base; pearly aperture.

SIZE: Length, 11 mm; width of base, 9 mm.

RANGE: Florida Gulf coast.

DESCRIPTION: Shell cone-shaped, imperforate, shoulder below center of whorl; whorls usually five and not curved; apex very pointed; sutures distinct; base nearly flat; aperture simple; umbilicus lacking; surface sculptured with finely beaded spiral lines—strongest beading at shoulder of whorl; alternate large and small beaded lines sculpture base. This tiny little top shell is easily distinguished from other species of the genus.

STAIRCASE SHELLS
Family EPITONIIDAE

This family of mollusks is widely distributed in all seas, but it is most abundant in the waters of the West Indies. Being carnivorous, the members prey upon the animal life which is so plentiful on sandy stations. They are commonly known as 'wentletraps' or 'staircase shells'.

The shells are usually a polished white and characterized by having many rounded, strongly ribbed whorls which gradually decrease in size from the base to the summit, thereby making the general shape turriculate.

Genus **EPITONIUM** Roeding, 1798

Humphrey's Staircase   Epitonium humphreysii Kiener

Plate XIV, Figures 3a, b

COLOR: Polished white.

SIZE: Length, 16-22 mm.

RANGE: Cape Cod to south Florida and in the Gulf of Mexico along the west coast of Florida to Texas.

DESCRIPTION: Shell solid, turret-shaped, imperforate; whorls seven to ten, decidedly convex, and connected to each other by elevated ribs (costae); suture deep; spire extended; aperture nearly circular; outer lip thickened; surface sculptured with many thickened, rounded —sometimes blade-like—ribs which may be slightly angled on shoulder of whorl.

This species is closely related to and often confused with E. angulatum. E. humphreysii is distinguished from the latter by its greater narrowness, more rounded ribs, and less developed shoulder angles.

CUP AND SAUCER LIMPETS
Family CALYPTRAEIDAE
Genus CALYPTRAEA Lamarck, 1799

Cup and Saucer Limpet   Calyptraea centralis Conrad
Plate XIV, Figures 4a, b

COLOR: Greyish-white exterior; glossy-white interior.

SIZE: Length, 5-10 mm.

RANGE: North Carolina to the Gulf of Mexico and up the west coast of Florida.

DESCRIPTION: Shell flattened, cap-shaped, fragile; summit spiral, pointed, slightly excentrical and tilted; base circular, sharp margined; sculpture consists of fine concentric basal lines and minute radial striae. One must watch closely to find these tiny little cap-shaped shells.

CONCH OR STROMB SHELLS
Family STROMBIDAE
Genus STROMBUS Linné, 1758

Ribbed Stromb   Plate XIV, Figures 5a, b   Strombus costatus Gmelin

COLOR: Exterior uniform creamy-white; interior, outer lip and columellar callus a porcelaneous white or cream color which often reflects a metallic luster; epidermis yellowish-brown.

SIZE: Length, 3-6 inches.

RANGE: Southeastern Florida through the West Indies.

DESCRIPTION: Shell large, robust, bluntly nodulose; about ten whorls which increase regularly in size up to the sharp spire; suture partially covers the knobs of whorl above; outer lip flared, usually thickened; aperture long; stromboid notch slightly developed near base of outer lip; anterior canal short and recurved; nuclear whorls are smooth but spire whorls are sculptured with conspicuous striations which become cord-like wavy ridges on the body whorl; spiral nodes are blunt, flat, and regularly spaced; four to six body whorl knobs are bluntly spinose. Specimens vary considerably in the matter of nodule development.

MUREX SHELLS
Family MURICIDAE
Genus MUREX Linné, 1758

Sand Rock Shell   Murex florifer arenarius Clench
Murex rufus (of authors)
Plate XIV, Figures 6a, b

COLOR: Ivory ground, pink apical whorls, fine brown lines which often become more densely grouped in region adjacent to varices give an additional color effect, spiny varices cream colored.

SIZE: Length, 1½-3½ inches.

RANGE: Florida Gulf coast and southeast coast.

DESCRIPTION: The topmost spine on each varix curves upward and is much larger than the other varical spines. Spaces between the varices are sculptured with a conspicuous nob and one or more axilary ridges. Varices extend nearly to base of canal. Spiral sculpture consists of raised ribs and interspacial threads. Anterior canal is nearly closed, recurved, expanded near base.

This is a new subspecies of M. florifer. According to present records it is limited to Florida, especially along the Gulf coast and southeast coast to the Keys.

Genus EUPLEURA H. and A. Adams, 1853
Ribbed Oyster Drill   Plate XIV, Figures 7a, b   Eupleura caudata Say

COLOR: Brown over-laid with greyish-white which in thickened varices and ribs is pure white.

SIZE: Length, 15-25 mm.

RANGE: Cape Cod to south Florida and Florida Gulf coast.

DESCRIPTION: Shell small, strong, about five whorls which are sharply angled at the shoulders; spire regularly tapered and acute; apex sharp; sutures well defined; body whorl looks curiously flattened because of the thickened varix on outer lip and one opposite on body whorl; aperture small, ovate; anterior canal straight, tapered, nearly closed; outer lip thickened and decorated on front with tiny nobs; conspicuous sculpture consists of sharp-edged, longitudinal ribs. The animal is white with a yellow foot.

Genus TRITONALIA Fleming, 1828
Little-Celled Murex   Plate XIV, Figures 8a, b   Tritonalia cellulosa Conrad

COLOR: Greyish-white exterior; light purple interior.

SIZE: Length, 19-29 mm.

RANGE: North Carolina to the Gulf of Mexico and south to the greater Antilles. It is only common along the Florida Gulf coast.

DESCRIPTION: Shell small, whorls moderately curved, five to seven channeled varices; spire tapered to point; aperture ovate and extended into a short, nearly closed, sharply recurved anterior canal;

former recurved anterior canals show as spiny terminations of the body whorl varices. In perfect, mature specimens, four growth canals are present. Varices are characteristically sculptured with strong revolving ridges between which are thread-like forms which produce a fluted effect; spiral sculpture overlaps axial ribs. This shell is very ornate for its size.

Family COLUBRARIIDAE

Genus COLUBRARIA Schumacher, 1817

Serpent's Lance   Plate XIV, Figures 9a, b   Colubraria lanceolata Menke

COLOR: Tan with a few spots of brown especially on varices; nuclear whorls chocolate-brown.

SIZE: Length, 20-25 mm.

RANGE: Florida east and west coasts south to the West Indies.

DESCRIPTION: Shell spindle-shaped, whorls five or six, body whorl over half the full height of shell; apex sharp; aperture elliptical; outer lip sharp-edged in front of a thickened varix; columellar callus erect and sharp-edged; canal short and slightly curved backward; whorls reticulated with fine axial ridges and minute spiral threads; varices one to two on each whorl. This gracefully shaped shell is easily identified.

DOVE SHELLS

Family PYRENIDAE

Genus PYRENE Roeding, 1798

Rustic Pyrene   Plate XIV, Figures 10a, b   Pyrene rusticoides Heilprin

COLOR: Greyish-white ground patterned with reddish-brown ripply streaks, reddish-brown interstices on outer lip and columella.

SIZE: Length, about 18 mm.

RANGE: Florida coasts to the West Indies.

DESCRIPTION: Shell smooth, ovate, spire short and pointed, body whorl about two-thirds height of shell; aperture long and slender; outer lip toothed and greatly thickened in center giving convex character; columella toothed below and curved to correspond with thickened outer lip; finely incised spiral striations on lower half of body whorl. The dark markings between teeth, smoother surface, and slightly larger size distinguish this species from P. mercatoria.

TOWER SHELLS

Family **TURRIDAE**

Genus **CRASSISPIRA** Swainson, 1840

Thick Coiled Tower   Crassispira tampaënsis Bartsch and Rehder

Plate XIV, Figures 11a, b

COLOR: Mahogany exterior, lavender interior.

SIZE: Length, 20-25 mm.

RANGE: North Carolina south and up the Gulf coast of Florida.

DESCRIPTION: Shell elongated, turret-shaped, strong, seven to nine whorls; apex pointed; suture channeled, a ridge above the channel clearly separates the whorls; aperture elongate-ovate; anterior canal short; outer lip with distinct notch near summit and slight stromboidal notch near base; whorls sculptured with many sharply angled, equidistant axial ridges which are crossed by fine thread-like striations thereby rendering the axial ridges slightly nodulose. This is a rather common shell which prefers moderately shallow water.

GLOSSARY OF DESCRIPTIVE TERMS

Adductor muscles . . . Muscles which fasten the bivalve animal to its shell.

Anterior canal . . . Downward extension of the aperture of an univalve shell.

Anterior end . . . The front of a living bivalve shell; the end of the shell to which the ligament is not attached.

Aperture . . . The opening of an univalve shell through which the animal extends itself.

Apex . . . Extreme top of univalve shells; the place where shell growth begins.

Auriform . . . Ear-shaped.

Axis . . . Imaginary central pillar of univalve shells around which the whorls are coiled.

Bilateral symmetry . . . Corresponding parts on either side of a median line of equal or balanced proportions.

Bivalve . . . Composed of two valves.

Body-whorl . . . See whorl.

Byssus . . . Thread-like filaments secreted by a gland in the animal's foot and used for attachment to objects.

Calcareous . . . Shell substance containing much calcium carbonate.

Callus . . . An enamel-like deposit often secreted on the columellar wall of some univalves.

Cancellated . . . Crossed or marked by horizontal and vertical lines which produce a lattice-like effect.

Cardinal teeth . . . Central tooth-like projections and depressions on the hinge margin.

Cirri . . . Slender, flexible appendages.

Columella . . . Central pillar of univalves extending from apex to base around which the whorls revolve.

Compressed . . . Flattened from side to side.

Concentric lines . . . Lines which follow the outline edges of bivalve shells.

Cordate . . . Heart-shaped.

Crenulated . . . Having the margins cut into minute, rounded scallops.

Deflected . . . Bent or turned backward or to the side.

Denticulate . . . Having tooth-like projections.

Dentated . . . Toothed.

Depressed spire . . . A spire which shows very little elevation above body-whorl.

Dextral . . . Having the opening or aperture on the right when the shell is held with the apex up.

Dorsal margin . . . Upper or hinge edge of bivalve shells.

Ears . . . Lateral projections on one or both sides of the umbones in some bivalves such as Pectens.

Elongated . . . Lengthened or stretched out.

Epidermis . . . Outer covering or skin of shells.

Equilateral . . . p. 21.

Equivalve . . . p. 21.

Escutcheon . . . A regularly shaped depression on the hinge margin posterior to the umbones which is found in some bivalves.

Foot . . . The ventral or under side of the animal's body on which the animal moves or rests when extended.

Fossette . . . A depressed, saucer-shaped shell structure just under the umbones inside the shell in some species of bivalves such as *Spisula solidissima similis.*

Fusiform . . . Spindle-shaped, tapering at either end.

Gaping . . . Bivalves are not entirely closed.

Globular . . . Rounded or globe-shaped.

Granulated . . . Surface roughened by the formation of small grain-like particles.

Herbivorous . . . Plant eating mollusks.

Hinge . . . Ligament and tooth structure of bivalves which hold the valves together.

Hinge teeth . . . Interlocking depressions and projections on the dorsal margin of bivalves.

Incremental lines . . . Lines which keep increasing.

Inequilateral . . . p. 21.

Inequivalve . . . p. 21

Inflated . . . Expanded or swollen.

Interstices . . . Spaces between raised parts of a shell.

Involute . . . Rolled inward at the edges.

Iridescent . . . Exhibiting rainbow colors.

Lamellate . . . Built up of folds or plates as in *Pinctada radiata.*

Lateral teeth . . . The outer-most teeth in the set of hinge teeth of a bivalve shell.

Left valve . . . p. 21.

Length . . . In bivalves, the measure from anterior to posterior end; in univalves, the measure from apex to base.

Ligament . . . A cartilaginous band of tissue on the dorsal margin of bivalve shells which assists in holding the valves together.

Lip, outer . . . Outer edge of the aperture in univalve shells.

Littoral region . . . That region which extends from the shore to a depth of about 100 fathoms.

Longitudinal . . . Pertaining to lengthwise direction.

Lunule . . . An impressed area—often heart-shaped—anterior of the umbones on the dorsal margin of some bivalves.

Mantle . . . A fleshy outgrowth or covering of the outer body wall.

Margin . . . Boundary or periphery of a shell.

Mouth . . . Opening or aperture of univalve shells.

Muricated . . . Equipped with sharp surface projections such as are found on some Murex shells.

Muscular impressions . . . Scars on the inside of bivalve shells which indicate where the adductor muscles were attached.

Nacreous . . . Pearly.

Nuclear whorls . . . First embryonic shell whorls.

Nodose . . . Knobby.

Oblique . . . Slanting between perpendicular and horizontal.

Operculum . . . A shelly or horny plate which closes the aperture of univalve shells when the animal is retracted.

Ovate . . . Egg-shaped; oval.

Pallial line . . . Impressed line on the inside of bivalve shells which is made by the attached mantle.

Pallial sinus . . . The siphon scar—a notch in the pallial line.

Papillaceous . . . Having warty outgrowths.

Parietal wall . . . Shell wall on the inside of the aperture.

Perforate . . . Said of the umbilicus of an univalve shell when it shows as a hole.

Plaits . . . Folds.

Plicate . . . Equipped with folds or plaits.

Porcelaneous . . . Resembling porcelain in translucent, enamel-like hardness.

Posterior canal . . . A notch at the upper extremity of the aperture in some univalves.

Posterior end . . . The back end of a living bivalve shell or end through which the siphons extend; the end of the shell nearest which the ligament is attached.

Pyriform . . . Pear-shaped.

Radiate markings . . . Sculpture or color line markings which spread out from a center.

Radiating lines . . . Lines on bivalves which radiate from the umbones out to the shell margin.

Radula . . . p. 51.

Recurved . . . Curved in the opposite direction.

Reflected . . . Bent, turned or directed back.

Reticulated . . . Said of shell surfaces on which lines are so crossed as to form a netted pattern.

Right valve . . . p. 21.

Scalloped . . . Having undulated edges.

Sculpture . . . Surface makings, elevated and impressed, of a shell.

Semilunar . . . Having the shape of a half moon.

Serrate . . . Finely notched on the edge like a saw edge.

Sinistral . . . Having the opening or aperture on the left when the shell is held with the apex up.

Sinuous . . . Curving in and out giving a wavy pattern.

Sinus . . . (see pallial sinus).

Siphon . . . A tubular structure or extended portion of the mantle-edge of molluscan animals.

Spiral . . . Coiled around a central axis.

Spirally striated . . . Having parallel, thread-like sculptural lines following the coiled direction of the shell whorls.

Spire . . . All the whorls of an univalve above the largest or body whorl.

Striae . . . Thread-like lines or fine bands.

Striated . . . Marked with thread-like sculptural lines.

Stromboid notch . . . A notch at the anterior end of the aperture in shells belonging to the family *Strombidae*.

Suture . . . Seam-like line formed by the union of the successive whorls of an univalve.

Symmetrical . . . Shells with sides equal in size and shape.

Teeth . . . In univalves, the tooth-like projections along the outer lip or on the columellar wall of some species. (See cardinal teeth and lateral teeth.)

Terminal . . . Pertaining to the end or extremity.

Testaceous . . . Having a hard shell.

Truncate . . . Having the end cut off.

Tubercles . . . Knob-like excrescences.

Turbinate . . . Shaped like a top or cone turned upside down.

Turriculate . . . Shaped like a turrent or tower.

Umbilicate . . . Having an umbilicus.

Umbilicus . . . A central pit extending from the base into the body-whorl of some species of univalves.

Umbo . . . The very highest point of each valve of a pelecypod shell; the place where the shell growth begins. It is usually anteriorly twisted.

Univalve . . . A mollusk shell having only one valve or part.

Varices . . . Greatly elevated ribs on univalve shells indicating rest periods and the position of former outer lips.

Varicose . . . Having irregular formations on the shell.

Varix . . . Sing. of varices.

Ventricose . . . Having swollen shell whorls.

Viviparous . . . Producing living young from within the body instead of eggs.

Whorl . . . One of the complete turns of a spiral shell. Body-whorl is the last and largest turn.

PLATES

PLATE I

PLATE I

PLATE II

EXPLANATION OF PLATE II
(Shells Natural Size)

PLATE II

2a

1

2c

2b

2d

7a

5a

6a

7b

5b

6b

3

5c

4

PLATE III

Explanation of Plate III

(Shells ½ Natural Size)

Figure   Page

PLATE III

PLATE IV

PLATE IV

PLATE V

PLATE V

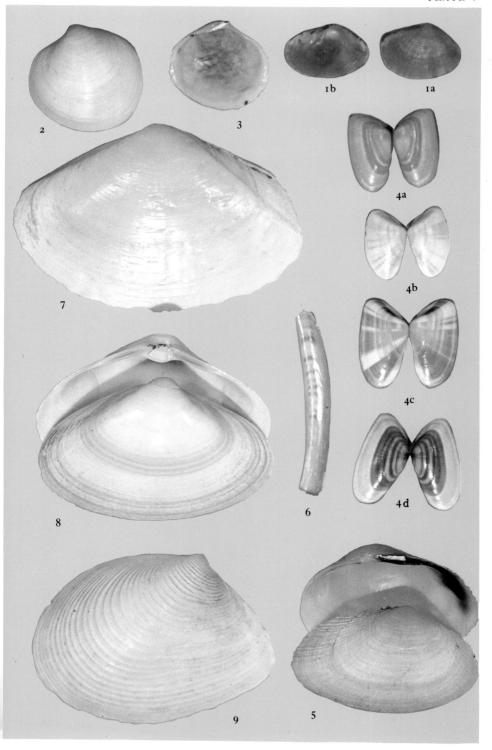

PLATE VI

PLATE VI

PLATE VII

EXPLANATION OF PLATE VII

(Shells ¾ Natural Size)

PLATE VII

PLATE VIII

PLATE VIII

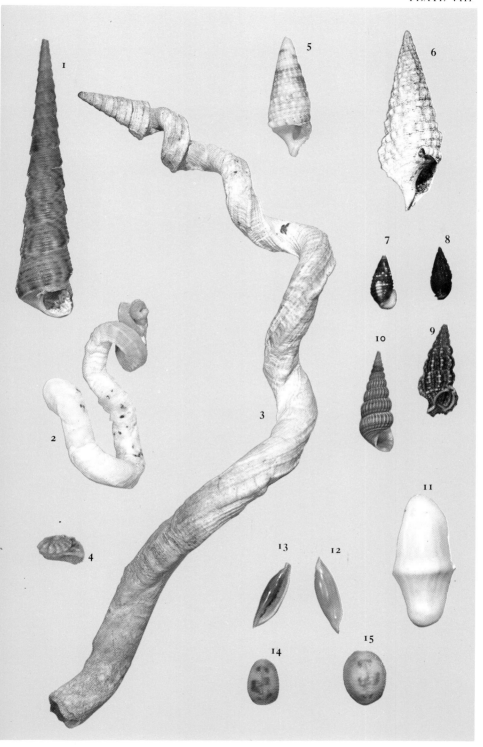

PLATE IX

EXPLANATION OF PLATE IX

(Shells ½ Natural Size)

PLATE IX

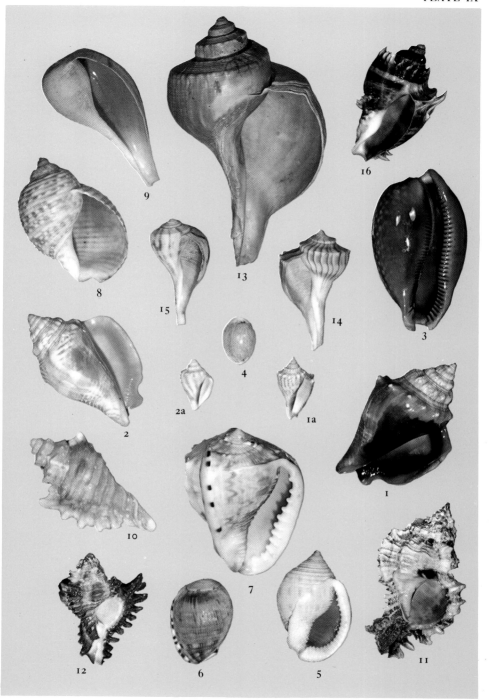

PLATE X

PLATE X

PLATE XI

PLATE XI

PLATE XII

PLATE XII

PLATE XIII

PLATE XIII

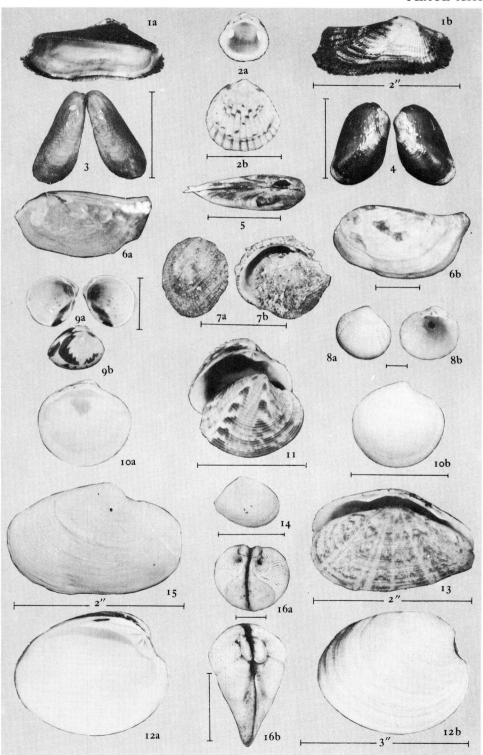

PLATE XIV

PLATE XIV

2a · 2b · 1 · 6a · 8a · 8b · 3a · 3b · 6'' · 6b · 9a · 9b · 4a · 4b · 5a · 10a · 10b · 7a · 7b · 5b · 11a · 11b

PLATE XIV

INDEX OF ENGLISH NAMES

Note: Roman numerals refer to the plate number;
arabic numerals refer to the page number.

- 165 -

INDEX OF ENGLISH NAMES (Continued)

INDEX OF LATIN NAMES

of

Classes, Families, Genera and Species